The Cover

The abstract cover design is intended to reflect the many facets and nuances of self-service analytics that make its design, implementation, and support a challenging proposition for most every organization.

EARLY ADOPTER RECOGNITION

In order to develop, write, and publish a book, an author needs the encouragement and enthusiasm that only a special group of people can provide. I call them Early Adopters—individuals who believe so much in an idea that they rally around it with early and significant support.

To my Early Adopters, thank you for helping me move this book from concept to reality. I am forever grateful.

William Bishop
Toby George
Angel Kahmar
Brian Lash
Alan Mann
Brian McCormac
Chris Miladinovich
Michael Onders
Donald Pavlinsky
Michael Yetter

PRAISE FOR THINK FAST!

"The use of data is defining new business models, disrupting industries and creating valuable experiences for consumers. While the outcomes can be transformative, the journey requires more than technical proficiency. Think Fast! can position your organization's operating model to scale its analytic driven transformation and compete against the next generation of disrupters."

Paul Hlivko
VP & CTO at Wellmark Blue Cross Blue Shield

"This book is the go-to bible in demystifying data analytics. I left reading this book with concrete, distinguishable takeaways in implementing a comprehensive BI environment for my clients' businesses. It is an easy read for even the busiest IT executive."

Robert Stein
Executive Director, Institute for Entrepreneurial Excellence at the University of Pittsburgh

"The technical skills needed to extract actionable insights from massive amounts of data are only one dimension to the analytics puzzle. In an increasingly competitive world where data science and analytics are being utilized across industries and platforms, Steffine re-introduces us to the peripheral skills that set apart the winners from the losers. Buy-in from the line of business, agility in development, making sure you meet the needs of the client (internal or external) are all key components that decide the success of a given analytics project, and this author does a fantastic job of identifying each component in the process. Think Fast! is an essential sidekick for any analytics professional looking to gain an edge above and beyond the tech stack."

Amir Biagi
Director of Data Science, AF Group

"Think Fast! sets early expectations and more crucially, stays true to them throughout, as an eminently-practical, conventional wisdom-challenging guide through the complexities and ever-shifting landscape of self-service analytics. Greg and his 'Perspectives from the Pros' colleagues cut to the core issues and tear down supposed 'truisms' found in many other analytics books that simply don't hold up to the realities of modern business. Particularly valuable to data-driven practitioners will be Think Fast's recognition of the people elements of the analytics equation, the oft-unrecognized linkage point between data and execution, as well as its well-integrated advice about the service models that make analytics sustainable and with optimized impact. Throughout the book, the context for analytics execution is never disconnected from the technical details of data science work. Technology receives a balanced treatment, with foundational definitions of key data concepts (including very timely themes of data privacy) reviewed, yet adeptly avoiding the trap of recommending technology that isn't firmly grounded in business purpose and company culture."

Evan Sinar, Ph.D.
Chief Scientist and Vice President, DDI

"Data is one of our most valuable assets, and self-service analytics can quickly get data into the hands of the people that can gain the most value from it. Think Fast! is a quick read that provides a lot of value on all aspects of what is needed for a successful self-service analytics ecosystem. I fully expect I will be referring to it often with my team."

Lisa Gardner
Data Analytics Architect

"In a new data world where even business executives are able to do their own analysis from complex company data, this book provides insight into all aspects of the people, processes, enabling technologies, and data and does so in a meaningful, easy to read format. Business intelligence professionals and partners are encouraged to rely on Think Fast! to help guide them to create higher value-driven programs using self-service analytics."

Alan Aguais
Global Program Manager, eBay, Inc.

"Think Fast! functions as a great self-service analytics primer for anyone — whether you are simply curious, tangentially involved, or responsible for creating and/or executing an enterprise strategy and looking for how to and how not to guidance."

Ian Gordon
Senior Vice President Operations, Regence Insurance Holding Company

"We have entered an era where immediacy is quickly becoming table stakes, technology is re-inventing industries and every company will be judged against the capabilities of all companies. Steffine's Think Fast! is a resource for leaders looking for best practices based on collective experiences and observations as to why organizations will succeed or fail in delivering meaningful insights that drive value and why it matters in this era of disruption."

Laura Gorry
Healthcare Executive, IBM Global Markets

"Think Fast! provides powerful guidelines that help IT eliminate the barriers that often hinder business analysts from achieving real results from data."

Andrew P. Hornyak
Sr. Business Intelligence Developer, University of Pittsburgh

"We all know how important deriving timely and actionable intelligence from data is for the success of any organization. Think Fast! introduces you to a simple but powerful business intelligence tool—self-service analytics—that does the job magnificently. The book helps you to think through all the critical nodes in its implementation to ensure its successful adoption at any organization."

Amit Marwah
Finance, Analytics and Risk Management Leader - Technology and Financial Services Industries

"At a time when analytics buzzwords and innovations are utilized regularly without thorough understanding of the concepts, Think Fast! helps leaders decipher the fundamentals of analytics with a simple approach to generating, evaluating, implementing, and maintaining sound strategies and offerings into varied organizations. This book navigates through the essentials to understanding data, provides a simplified mechanism to creating an analytics culture, and shares the principles for integrating analytics processes and tools. Steffine delivers insightful knowledge in an easy to read narrative while the inputs from experienced pros add relevant expertise and useful insights. Now more than ever, leaders need to leverage knowledgeable data and reliable business intelligence to ensure sound decision-making for staying current and successful. An excellent resource to keep on hand, Think Fast! will help any leader be more effective in their analytics endeavors."

Era Prakash
Product Leadership and Strategy Consultant

"Think Fast! is an insightful must-read for any BI Professional trying to define and lead an agile analytics organization. It provides a well-balanced and clear perspective on self-service analytics. This is especially relevant in today's world where the nature and volume of data being produced from various sources can provide fresh insights and value to the organization."

Arun Raju
VP Enterprise Architecture - Global Corporate Platforms, Equifax

"Think Fast! presents invaluable insight into delivering effective analytics capability to the end user. I'm using Greg's methods and suggestions on my next BI project."

John Zeiner
Manager Risk Analytics and Payment Innovation, Gateway Health

"In my experience with the world's leading companies, I've found that the key differentiators for building best-in-class products and services are a commitment to design thinking and an adherence to business intelligence best practices. Greg Steffine delivers a primer on the latter in Think Fast! Powerful, thoughtful and engaging, this edition will hold a place on my office bookshelf for years to come—right next to his award-winning book, Hyper!"

Dan Grace
SVP and Director - Innovation Product Management, Bank of America

"Think Fast! delivers an easy-to-understand approach with different perspectives to help you be successful with self-service analytics. This book guides BI professionals and managers to improve their existing environments to create analytical results fast(er)."

Dr. Tobias S. Witte
President & Founder of Wittbix LLC, Business Intelligence Executive

think
fast!

THE INSIGHT YOU NEED TO COMPETE AND WIN WITH
self-service analytics

GREGORY P. STEFFINE

FOREWORD BY BORIS EVELSON

Sanderson

Sanderson℠

Published by Sanderson Press, LLC
P.O. Box 1373, Aliquippa, Pennsylvania 15001-9998
United States

Think Fast! The insight you need to compete and win
with self-service analytics

ISBN: 978-1-7320108-0-2

DEDICATION

To Mary
Thank you for your love and unconditional support.

To Jonathan, Aaron, Daniel, and Abigail
Always remember, the Lord has a special plan for your life.

To Sandy and Leo
You'll always be my best friends.

To my colleagues and friends
Thank you for enabling me to do what I love.

To Rock and the entire team at UPMC
You're the best at what you do. I'm blessed to be under your care.

To my Lord and Savior, Jesus Christ
Thank you for all of your blessings, including the promise of John 3:16 and the assurance of Jeremiah 29:11. I pray that my work is honoring in your sight.

TABLE OF CONTENTS

CONTRIBUTORS

MIKE SARGO

Mr. Sargo is a proven business intelligence and analytics leader with nearly two decades of experience architecting and delivering enterprise data management solutions. Prior to co-founding Data Ideology—a boutique consultancy focused on helping customers maximize the value of their data—Mike led large, cross-industry enterprise deployments of business intelligence solutions for Oracle and Microsoft. See Mike's LinkedIn profile at linkedin.com/in/mikesargo.

SRI SEEPANA

Mr. Seepana is a business intelligence and analytics professional with over 18 years of experience in e-commerce, financial services, healthcare, and research. He currently serves as Manager of Analytics and Reporting at a leading e-commerce company. He has contributed to several research publications in price analysis, marketing, and analytics technologies. You can find him on LinkedIn at linkedin.com/in/sriseepana.

ABHI SINDHWANI, MHA, MCSD

Abhishek (Abhi) Sindhwani has been a healthcare analytics visionary since 2006. For more than 20 years he's focused on the use of business intelligence and analytics to address the shifting business paradigms that impact the bottom line. Abhi helps healthcare insurers improve their clinical operations, network management, and consumer engagement while minimizing provider abrasion. You can connect with him on LinkedIn at linkedin.com/in/abhisindhwani.

FOREWORD

TAKE YOUR BI ENVIRONMENT TO THE NEXT LEVEL BY BUILDING A SYSTEM OF INSIGHT

Many executives aspire to make their business insights-driven; that is, capable of harnessing and implementing data and analytics to drive growth and create differentiating products and services. Yet a preoccupation with collecting and mining data means they often fall short of this goal. While these "data-aware" or "data-driven" firms detect signals in their business intelligence (BI) applications, they struggle to translate these learnings into tangible business outcomes. Why? Because insights-driven companies are fundamentally different from other firms as they[1]

- have operating models based on insights;
- harness insights from various sources and implement them in software;
- have a culture that promotes innovation and continuous learning;
- make strategic data, analytics and insights investments;
- build cross-functional teams that are accountable for business outcomes.

---

[1] Hopkins, Brian, James McCormick, and Ted Schadler. "Insights-Driven Businesses Set The Pace For Global Growth." Forrester Research, Inc. 18 Oct 2017. (http://goo.gl/4tghz7).

BI is a key foundational component of an insights-driven organization, but only if it equips decision-makers to quickly and easily analyze data and act on derived insights. Forrester views "systems of insight" as that solution and natural evolution of BI. We define it as:

> The business discipline and technology to harness insights and consistently turn data into action.

This approach combines all the BI best practices to address the limitations of earlier systems, like information silos, costliness, complexity and inflexibility. In an insights-driven business, technology and business professionals work together to design and build systems of insight. As you begin to think about your plans, keep in mind the five capabilities that characterize this modern BI environment:[2]

1. Designed to encourage self-service

Systems of insight must empower business users—those closest to customer problems, market shifts or operational inefficiencies—to experiment, collaborate and generate insights on their own.[3] They're the ones in the best position to make informed decisions that improve business outcomes. Specifically, platforms must have features that help business pros: a) provision their own BI applications and data sets; b) perform some data integration and data mashup tasks within the environment; c) automate BI, ridding it of manual steps; d)

---

[2] Evelson, Boris. "It's Time To Upgrade Business Intelligence To Systems Of Insight." Forrester Research, Inc. 3 Jan. 2017. (http://goo.gl/pL4YdS).
[3] Evelson, Boris. "It's Time For A User-Driven Enterprise BI Strategy." Forrester Research, Inc. 25 Aug. 2014. (http://goo.gl/aY7scD).

make information exploration and discovery more effective and intuitive; and e) use data visualizations to drive additional analysis. Providing business users with a sandbox to generate BI content and a shared environment to collaborate and leverage each other's work lends itself well to an agile process for determining what eventually becomes productionized in enterprise systems.

2. Embedded in operational applications

Embedding business intelligence content into ERP, CRM, and other transactional applications delivers relevant information to users within the systems they rely on every day.[4] It becomes pervasive. For example, you can display supplier inventory levels, current prices and delivery times right inside an inventory management system. This schema also has the added benefit of eliminating the complexities of finding the right data sources, metrics and attributes, since it carries context from an external application—and takes the user right to the relevant data.

3. Connected to an execution engine

The future BI environment seamlessly integrates with a company's systems of engagement for all customer touch-points, systems of record for transactional processing, and systems of automation for all physical processes. This architecture allows users to immediately act on an insight within an operational application, i.e., bridge the insights-to-execution gap. For example, with a system of insight, instead

---

[4] Evelson, Boris, and John R. Rymer. "The New Generation Of Embedded BI Will Close The Insights-To-Action Gap." Forrester Research, Inc. 11 Apr. 2017. (http://goo.gl/wNmidG).

of a dashboard just flashing red to indicate low inventory, a dialog box could pop up that a procurement manager can use to place a purchase order or initiate a purchase order approval process. Some platforms offer out-of-the box features to automatically trigger a workflow or compare the potential outcomes of different actions.

4. Architected to support continuous improvement

Gone are the days of relying on intuition and subjective assessment of business users' satisfaction to measure BI effectiveness. Technologists need "BI on BI" tools that mine data warehouse and data mart database logs as well as BI usage metadata to understand usage patterns. Building a closed-loop system that continuously measures what dashboards, queries or visualizations business pros use and the outcome of applied insights is key to optimizing and streamlining BI platforms, tools, and applications. Insights driven businesses instrument every process to constantly learn and adapt faster than their peers.[5]

5. Built or stored in alternative database management platforms

While highly curated enterprise data warehouses will always have a place in business intelligence, systems of insight allow business decision makers to access and derive value from all transactional data sets, including unstructured ones. Technologist can now look to machine learning-based automated data discovery, semantic data catalogs, data warehouse automation tools and data preparation tools to

---

[5] Evelson, Boris. "Divide (BI Governance From Data Governance) And Conquer. Forrester Research, Inc. 4 Jan. 2017. (http://goo.gl/npyJ83).

programmatically build analytic repositories for use cases that don't require a single version of the truth. These artificial intelligence-enabled tools help users derive insights and make decisions based on a truly complete view of customers and products.

Forrester recommends our BI Playbook[6] and The Insight-Driven Business Playbook[7] to help your organization understand the roadmap, strategy and success factors for a data, analytics and insights transformation. Then turn to Think Fast! to jump-start and energize your effort with the kind of pragmatic advice that only comes from years of hands-on field work.

Boris Evelson
Vice President and Principal Analyst
Forrester Research, Inc.

Elizabeth Cullen
Researcher
Forrester Research, Inc.

---

[6] "The Business Intelligence Playbook For 2018: Drive Business Insight With Effective BI Strategy." Forrester Research, Inc., 2018. (http://goo.gl/F4VgfK).

[7] "The Insights-Driven Business Playbook." Forrester Research, Inc., 2018. (http://goo.gl/TjTuQE).

PREFACE

We are living in an age of accelerating disruption. That means every organization, regardless of industry or company size, is under intense pressure to create value. It's critical that business leaders can take what they know and turn it into action in order to compete and win. I like how McKinsey describes it. "Disruptive times call for transformational leaders with a knack for solving complex [business] problems."[8] That's where analytics comes in.

Analytics brings together business acumen and the science of numbers in order to find meaning in data. Business leaders need actionable insight to transform their organizations—to innovate, differentiate, and compete.

The objective of self-service analytics is to create value from data by leveraging the intellectual capital and untapped curiosity of the enterprise.

The idea began years ago when departments like sales, marketing, and finance felt a growing urgency to separate themselves from complete reliance on IT. Back then, most organizations staffed centralized reporting teams within information technology because complex operational systems weren't easy to navigate. They required a level of technical expertise to understand the underlying data models, and they required programming skills to generate reports. With the advent of the data warehouse and user-friendly reporting tools that

---

[8] Bourton, Sam, Johanne Lavoie, and Tiffany Vogel. "Leading with inner agility" *McKinsey Quarterly*. Mar. 2018. (http://goo.gl/TkDqH1).

incorporated semantic layers to shield users from underlying database complexities, the movement to self-service began. It was the ever-increasing market pressure to drive results at a faster and faster pace that ultimately put business and IT at odds.

Business leaders who once viewed IT as an enabler of innovation and transformation began to see the organization as a roadblock to the kind of responsiveness it required to generate results. IT leaders began to see business stakeholders as unreasonable and unwilling to accept the kind of thoughtful rigor required to make solutions perform and last. As time passed and technology evolved, so did their thinking. Today, self-service has become the model for empowering business leaders with access to data and technology they need to power analytics. It's also a key component in helping to bring Forrester's vision of the insights driven enterprise to life.

Think Fast! is the sequel to my award-winning book, Hyper. This time I've teamed-up with other experienced pros to condense years of hands-on field work into the 26 insights you need to think about to make self-service analytics really work. This book is an extension of our collective work, so in it you'll find the same ideas we've developed and honed over the course of our careers to help build smarter organizations.

Think Fast! is not a technical resource on how to architect, deploy, or govern a self-service environment. It assumes you or your colleagues already know how to do that. Rather, it focuses on what we believe are the most important and often forgotten aspects of people, processes, technology, and data necessary for self-service success.

The book is organized into six sections:

Section I - Understanding Self-Service Analytics
This section provides an overview of analytics, presents a foundational understanding of self-service, and covers its value-creation objective.

Section II - The People Domain
People represent an organization's greatest source of competitive advantage. In Section II we cover organizational alignment, the importance of collaboration, and discuss the team make-up you need to be successful with self-service analytics.

Section III - The Process Domain
In this section my contributors and I focus on setting priorities, balancing risk and reward, ways to sell your vision, and the importance of controlling the chaos that can often result from self-service.

Section IV -The Technology Domain
Technology plays an important role in making self-service analytics work. In this section we discuss the right architecture, we talk about the place for big data, and we cover the crowded and often confusing analytics landscape.

Section V - The Data Domain
Self-service analytics would not exist without data. In Section V we help you understand some of the important nuances of data including how to prepare it, the science behind it, and critical privacy concerns.

Section VI - Closing Thoughts
In Section VI I leave you with some closing thoughts on effective planning and execution and the importance of a mindset that embraces change.

Think Fast! is intended for busy business and IT professionals who have responsibility for building and growing a self-service analytics capability, and for those folks responsible for utilizing it to drive more effective decision-making.

Lastly, I'm often asked about the title of my books. This time I settled on "think fast" (and included an exclamation point!) because, in my experience, too many organizations and the practitioners who execute their analytics initiatives think and act too slow.

Fact is, our world is obsessed with speed, and an organization's survival ultimately rests on how well and fast it creates value.

To compete and win, the disruptive and demanding nature of business requires that we change the way we think. It's my hope that this book helps you make the important and necessary shift in mindset.

To your success.

Gregory P. Steffine
Business Intelligence Strategist and Solution Delivery Leader

Acknowledgements

Writing a book is a monumental undertaking, and it simply wouldn't be possible without extensive help from a lot of folks.

To Boris Evelson
Your wisdom always helps to challenge and clarify my thinking. Thank you.

To my contributors
Thank you for your insight. Your perspectives add valuable color for our readers.

To my peer review group
To Mike Betts, Joliene Garlich, Doug Lauffler, and Pooja Mehta—your constructive feedback was immensely helpful. Thank you for investing your time in my work.

To my editorial team
To Paul Hlivko, Robert Stein, Amir Biagi, Evan Sinar, Lisa Gardner, Alan Aguais, Ian Gordon, Laura Gorry, Andrew Hornyak, Amit Marwah, Era Prakash, Arun Raju, John Zeiner, Dan Grace, and Dr. Tobias Witte. Thank you for your pre-read and thoughtful comments.

To my partners
To John Matusin, Ronald van Loon, Brent Dykes, and Chart Mogul—thank you for sharing your intellectual capital.

SECTION I

UNDERSTANDING SELF-SERVICE ANALYTICS

INSIGHT [1]

VALUE ATTAINMENT

THE POINT: ORGANIZATIONS EXIST TO CREATE VALUE

Every organization today, regardless of industry or company size, faces the challenging mandate of competing more effectively. "Sell more, spend less" is the business edict, and the process of working smarter is more important now than ever before. That's why for the last 11 out of 13 years now, business leaders have consistently ranked business intelligence (think reporting and analytics) as their top investment priority. They recognize the instrumental role information plays in helping drive innovation. They understand the significance of information in creating differentiation. And they know the importance of information in monitoring and managing performance. In short, they rely on information to compete. For these business leaders and the firms they manage, reporting and analytics enable value creation.

Creating value is taking what you know and turning it into action in order to achieve a desired business outcome. Value outcomes often take the form of action words like increase, reduce and strengthen; grow, shrink and improve; maximize, minimize and revitalize. Creating value, says author and business advisor Jill

Konrath, is all about movement.[9] In one of its recent market reports,[10] E&Y states that high-performance organizations share something in common when it comes to creating movement, and that something is accelerated decision-making. Value creation depends on it. When the process of moving from great idea to actionable insight is fast and focused, it represents one of the most significant differences between top performing organizations and those who want to be. Results-based leaders see information as the lifeblood of business, and they recognize the instrumental role insight plays in delivering high-performance.

As you work to create value, keep in mind three Value-Enabling Rules:

Value-Enabling Rule #1 - Data must be relevant
Effective analytics begins with the identification of data that helps to strengthen the decision-making process. That said, we live in an era of information overload. Don't flood business users with useless data.

Value-Enabling Rule #2 - Information must be meaningful
Meaningful information is useful information because it's accurate, consistent, and relevant to business need. Information that doesn't impart knowledge is just noise.

Value-Enabling Rule #3 - Insight must be actionable
Information becomes actionable when it imparts important knowledge and provides an opportunity for decision-makers to act in a way that makes an impact.

---

[9] Konrath, Jill. *Value Proposition Generator*. (http://goo.gl/3BYFCM).
[10] Ernst & Young. "Lessons from Change: Findings from the Market." *EYGM Limited*, 2010. (http://goo.gl/g73XMR).

Impact is the objective.

In the late 90s, Richard Connelly, Robin McNeill, and Roland Mosimann—pioneers in the development of business intelligence technology and applications—authored a small paperback book distributed by Cognos called, *The Multidimensional Manager: 24 ways to impact your bottom line in 90 days*. The book provides practical insight into the critical importance of mastering information in order to make an impact. "Unlike many ideas for improving performance," the authors write, "the 24 Ways do not require you to declare a revolution in your company, change your leadership style, foster a new culture by edict, or consciously set out to reengineer the way people behave." Rather, the authors understood the significance of data and the role analytics plays in changing the way corporations operate and create value. See Figure 1.1 for an overview of the 24 Ways.

In its Total Economic Impact™ framework for BI, Forrester calls out 6 categories of potential value you should consider:[11]
- Cost savings (from automating manual processes)
- Top- and bottom-line benefits
- Increased value of assets
- Decreased capital requirements
- Risk avoidance
- BI as a profit center

Deloitte's *The Value Habit*[12] discusses the value-creating behaviors that close the gap between what you know and what you do. Test your organization's passion for value creation by pondering the five key questions they pose:

---

[11] Evelson, Boris and Martha Bennett. "Quantify The Tangible Business Value of BI." Forrester Research, Inc. 10 Jan. 2018. (http://goo.gl/9qzMrH).
[12] "The Value Habit: A Practical Guide for Creating Value." Straight Talk Book No. 6. Deloitte Development LLC. (2005).

FINANCE	HR/IT	SALES	MARKETING	PURCHASING	PRODUCTION	DISTRIBUTION	SERVICE
Multidimensional Income Statement	HR Administration	Sales Analysis	Strategic Marketing Analysis	Inventory Turnover	Capacity Management	Carrier Scorecard	On-Time Delivery
Profit Drill-Down Analysis	Core Competence Inventory	Customer and Product Profitability	Tactical Marketing Analysis	Supplier Scorecard	Standard Product Cost & Quality		Complaints, Returns and Claims
Multidimensional Balance Sheet	BI Deployment	Sales Plan vs. Forecast			Cause of Poor Quality		Cost of Service Relationship
Key Financial Ratios	24 Ways ROI	Sales Pipeline					
Cash Flow Analysis							

Figure 1.1 - 24 Ways to Impact Your Business

1. How do you define value in your company?
2. How do you create value for your stakeholders?
3. How do you manage the value-creation process?
4. How well do you align business strategies and initiatives?
5. Do you reward value-creating performance?

Gartner summarizes it this way: your analytics strategy must evolve from being just a *contributor* to business change to something that actually *provokes business transformation.*

PERSPECTIVES FROM THE PROS

Mike Sargo

Organizations produce more data today at faster rates than ever before. The resulting "data explosion" is creating incredible opportunities for forward-thinking leaders to create value by literally transforming the way they do business. That's important because disruption—from market volatility to regulation and security threats—is wreaking havoc on business. Leaders need to figure out how to better compete. Those who invest in analytics find ways to differentiate their organizations, create strategic advantage, and ultimately deliver value.

Sri Seepana

The ability to create demonstrable value is the driving force in most analytics efforts. In my experience, value often takes the form of cost avoidance, real cost reduction, or revenue enhancement. Value can take the form of productivity gains or process efficiencies, too. The important thing is to define an expected measurable return that can be used to help establish the right priorities when you inevitably encounter competing interests for limited investment dollars.

Abhi Sindhwani

Healthcare is one industry where value creation is increasingly dependent on putting the right information into the right hands at the right time. Historically, business intelligence and analytics platforms created artificial barriers between insurers, providers, and patients by delivering insights tailored to their individual needs. Healthcare insurers focused on their financials. Providers focused on quality of care and outcomes. And patients often relied on disparate data from whatever source to help make decisions about their care. Today, we're in an era of collaboration across the entire healthcare continuum, and that collaboration is delivering unprecedented value for all three stakeholder communities.

THE TAKEAWAY

Remember that the value of any analytics initiative is ultimately determined by the insight it provides and the impact it helps create. Building a report, a fancy dashboard, or a sophisticated model is a waste of valuable time if it doesn't generate actionable insight. Your job is to help your organization create value. Think of ways to turn data into information and information into actionable insight. Understand the process your business leaders go through to make decisions, and work overtime to support them with the insight they need when they need it. For help establishing expected outcomes and measuring value creation, consider the 24 Ways. And turn to tools like Forrester's Business Intelligence Playbook, Deloitte's Enterprise Value Map, or the Gartner Business Value Model.

INSIGHT [2]

AGILE BI

THE POINT: ORGANIZATIONS HAVE TO BE QUICK AND NIMBLE

Our world is obsessed with speed, and every business needs to think and move faster than its competition if it's going to survive. As writer and PR consultant Tom Clive puts it, "Dinosaurs must learn to become pumas."[13]

Now, more than ever, business leaders need access to the right information at the right time in order to act before decision windows close. That's important because, as research by Accenture indicates, organizations with the ability to quickly convert data to information to business value enjoy a significant competitive advantage over those who can't. It's what separates the best from the rest.

Agile BI (agile with a small A) is an approach to analytics that enables organizations to work in quick, iterative cycles to define

---

[13] Clive, Tom. "The Importance of Business Agility." *The Huffington Post*. 24 Apr. 2013. (http://goo.gl/n8wWj1).

and deliver a business-aligned analytics capability over time, one incremental step at a time. TechTarget points out that an agile methodology anticipates the need for flexibility and applies important pragmatism to the design and development of analytics solutions. As a solutions delivery leader, I can't stress enough the importance of that statement. In my award-winning book, Hyper,[14] I outline an accelerated approach to the planning and delivery of analytics solutions using an agile mindset.

In its Agile Organization series, McKinsey outlines the five trademarks and 23 practices of an agile organization.[15] "The trademarks," its authors write, "include a network of teams within a people-centered culture that operates in rapid learning and fast decision cycles with are enabled by technology, and a common purpose that co-creates value for all stakeholders." McKinsey's perspective on organizational agility goes well beyond analytics, for sure; however, the trademarks they outline certainly apply to the world of agile BI. Read up on them—especially since research by McKinsey shows that agile organizations "achieve greater customer centricity, faster time to market, higher revenue growth, lower costs, and a more engaged workforce"[16] than their non-agile counterparts.

Whether or not you adopt formal agile methodologies, your focus must be on fast, frequent releases of self-service BI capabilities. Think hours and days, not weeks or months. What Klaus Schwab said a number of years ago at the Davos World Economic Forum still holds true today: "We've moved from a world where the big

---

[14] Steffine, Gregory P. *Hyper: Changing the way you think about, plan, and execute business intelligence for real results, real fast!* Sanderson Press, 2015. (ISBN: 978-0-6924230-8-0).

[15] Aghina, Wouter, Aaron De Smet, Gerald Lackey, Et.al. "The five trademarks of agile organizations." *McKinsey Quarterly.* Jan. 2018.

[16] Ibid.

eat the small to a world where the fast eat the slow." The pace of business is only increasing. Your analytics capability—and the mindset you use to implement it—needs to keep up.

PERSPECTIVES FROM THE PROS

Mike Sargo

The business intelligence market has evolved to a point where organizations can now deliver solutions in an agile way, enabling business users to access the data they need when they need it as business needs change. No longer does the business have to rely on IT to manage and respond to report requests. Instead, technology professionals can focus their efforts and expertise on data management and governance. This transformational shift is the key to unlocking the full potential of an agile business intelligence deployment.

Sri Seepana

Agile BI is about being "entrepreneurial." Successful entrepreneurs focus on the journey, not the destination. BI initiatives are a journey. Unlike technology projects, they have no end date. Instead, they evolve as the business evolves. The entrepreneurial mindset empowers a leader to quickly translate an idea into action, and then learn from the experience and iterate. That's how effective agile BI efforts operate. Fail fast is the entrepreneur's mantra, and so it is with agile BI.

Abhi Sindhwani

In the healthcare industry, any methodology you adopt must keep the patient front and center. Agile, whether formally or informally implemented, provides a valuable framework that enables payers and providers alike to quickly test new ideas without large investments and without affecting care delivery or management. In fact, for years now the healthcare industry has been leveraging business intelligence and analytics to deliver more efficient care, to provide better patient experience, and to reduce the cost and service burden on providers; agile has been an important part of the equation.

THE TAKEAWAY

When you think agile BI, think speed-to-value. After all, agility only matters if it helps your organization to sell more, spend less, or work smarter. Look for ways to move your organization from big idea to actionable insight in a fast, focused manner. Partner with business stakeholders to identify high-value, low-risk opportunities that can help jumpstart your analytics effort. Don't overcomplicate things. Being agile means keeping things simple. Start with data that is readily available and accessible. And when it comes to data quality, don't let perfect be the enemy of good enough.

INSIGHT [3]

DEFINING ANALYTICS

THE POINT: ANALYTICS IS A JOURNEY TO VALUE ATTAINMENT

Wikipedia defines analytics as "the discovery, interpretation, and communication of meaningful patterns in data."[17] TechTarget describes it as "the science of examining raw data with the purpose of drawing conclusions about that information."[18] And Gartner says that "Analytics has emerged as a catch-all term for a variety of different business intelligence (BI)- and application-related initiatives."[19]

To me, analytics is the process of exploring data for the purpose of uncovering actionable insight that ultimately improves decision-making. It falls under the umbrella of "business intelligence." Analytics combines business acumen with the science of numbers to find meaning in data. Analytics is a journey to value attainment.

---

[17] "Analytics." *Wikipedia*. (http://goo.gl/XG2wN6).
[18] "Data Analytics." *SearchDataManagement*. (http://goo.gl/c88d6y).
[19] "Analytics." Gartners, Inc. (http://goo.gl/w5zrvy).

Talk to most practitioners and they'll agree on four types of analytics I present in Figure 3-1:

1. **Descriptive analytics** answers the question, "*What happened?*" It describes the past. Because it looks at historical data, the purpose of descriptive analytics is to understand business performance after the fact. When you think about descriptive analytics, think descriptions, comparisons, and categorization. Descriptive analytics uses descriptive statistics like counts, sums, averages, and percentage change to report on a company's operations and financial performance. In fact, you'll find a lot of descriptive analytics in traditional operational reporting.

2. **Diagnostic analytics** answers the question, "*Why* did it happen?" It examines historical data in order to develop insight into past events. While descriptive analytics describes past business performance, the purpose of diagnostic analytics is to determine what conditions, factors, or events actually affected that performance. Diagnostic analytics looks at inference, pattern detection, and causal relationships.

3. **Predictive analytics** answers the question, "What *will* happen?" Unlike descriptive analytics and diagnostic analytics, predictive analytics is forward-looking. It focuses on the identification of trends and patterns in historical data to reliably forecast future trends and business performance.

4. **Prescriptive analytics** is the most advanced form of analytics and answers the question, "What should I *do*?" Prescriptive analytics focuses on identifying optimal

recommendations and establishing the best course of action for a given situation. Among its business drivers are greater customer insight, risk management, and channel execution in financial services; improved personalization and engagement, pricing optimization, and inventory management in retail; and improved real-time alerting and patient care in healthcare.

Descriptive and diagnostic analytics are generally categorized as "business analytics." That is, they focus on monitoring and measuring business performance using *descriptive statistics*. These are the types of analytics most prevalent in organizations today and the natural starting point for firms at the beginning of their analytics journey. It's in these areas where you'll find line of business analysts using traditional reporting platforms and newer data visualization tools.

On the other end of the analytics journey you find predictive and prescriptive analytics. They fall under a category known as "quantitative analytics." Quantitative analytics uses *inferential statistics* to understand, estimate, predict, and prescribe behavior. The focus here is optimization, and the skillsets and technology required are much more sophisticated and complex. This is the area where you'll find an organization's specialized analytics talent often referred to as data scientists. They'll have advanced degrees in fields like computer science, math and statistics, engineering, and operations. And they'll be adept at modeling using a variety of languages and technologies like R, Python, SAS, and Java.

For most organizations today, quantitative analytics is aspirational. Their current analytics capability is either immature, or they struggle to overcome the cost and complexity barriers that often make predictive and prescriptive analytics challenging to operationalize. Others have achieved a mature analytics capability, especially in data- and analytics-rich industries like retail, healthcare, and financial services. For them, the analytics journey is over, and there is little distinction between business and quantitative analytics. "We see it as an analytics spectrum," says Michael Onders, Chief Data Officer for KeyBank, one of the nation's largest bank-based financial services firms. "We've built competency across all four types of analytics, and we tap into whatever capabilities we need across the spectrum to help improve customer-centricity, drive revenue growth, reduce cost, and better manage risk."

It's a point of view that aligns well with the way Forrester Research sees analytics.

"Many wrongly and incompletely define prescriptive analytics as what comes after predictive analytics," writes analyst Mike Gualtieri. "Our research indicates that prescriptive analytics is not a specific type of analytics, but rather an umbrella term for many types of analytics that can improve decisions. Think of the term 'prescriptive' as the goal of all these analytics—to make more effective decisions—rather than a specific analytical technique."[20]

The Cambridge, Massachusetts-based research firm defines predictive analytics as "Any combination of analytics, math, experiments, simulation, and/or artificial intelligence used to improve the effectiveness of decisions made by humans or by decision logic embedded in applications." It includes streaming

---

[20] Gualtieri, Mike. "What Exactly Heck Are Prescriptive Analytics?" *Build An Insights-Driven Org Blog.* Forrester Research, Inc. 5 Jun. 2018. (http://goo.gl/5GmBZM).

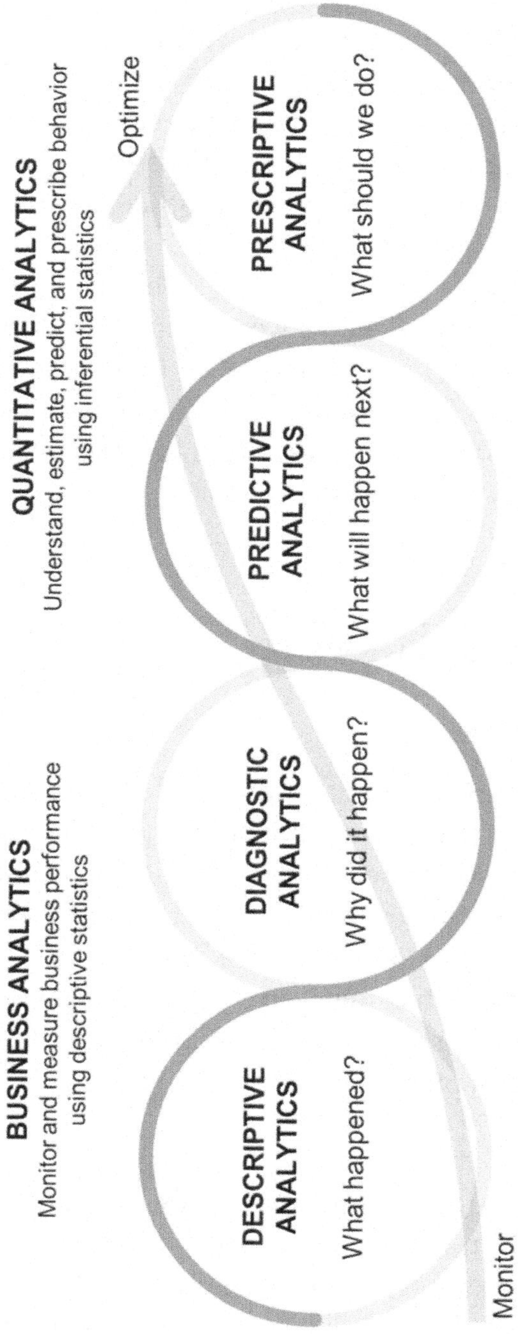

BUSINESS ANALYTICS
Monitor and measure business performance using descriptive statistics

QUANTITATIVE ANALYTICS
Understand, estimate, predict, and prescribe behavior using inferential statistics

Optimize

Monitor

DESCRIPTIVE ANALYTICS
What happened?

DIAGNOSTIC ANALYTICS
Why did it happen?

PREDICTIVE ANALYTICS
What will happen next?

PRESCRIPTIVE ANALYTICS
What should we do?

Figure 3.1 - The Analytics Journey

analytics, search and knowledge discovery, simulation, mathematical optimization, machine learning, and pragmatic AI. It's an interesting perspective, but I'm not sure the distinction Forrester makes is all that important—especially given the industry's long-held view that I described earlier. One thing is for sure, though: no matter how you define it, business leaders recognize the instrumental role analytics plays in helping to improve business performance. Just keep in mind that, as technology evolves and vendors work to embed more and more advanced capabilities into their tools (like Tableau acquiring MIT AI spinoff Empirical Systems and natural language query startup ClearGraph), the line between traditional business analytics and quantitative analytics will continue to blur.

PERSPECTIVES FROM THE PROS

Mike Sargo

I use the term analytics to describe, at a macro level, all of the activities required to deliver actionable insight to business users. These activities represent important components of an organization's analytics strategy, I might even include big data and advanced topics like machine learning and predictive modeling. When it comes to delivering analytics, the objective is to help determine what happened, establish why it happened, and predict what will happen next.

Sri Seepana

Analytics is a very broad term that infers lots of things depending on the audience. To a software engineer, for example, analytics focuses on the extraction, transformation and loading (ETL) of data from multiple sources into a unified, presentable format.

Statisticians, on the other hand, view the concept of analytics from a modeling perspective, connecting multiple variables or factors to determine historical patterns and predictive forecasts. In my opinion, it's important to expose yourself to diverse groups of stakeholders to help you understand the nuances of a term that has varying meanings.

Abhi Sindhwani

I think analytics is one of the most over-used terms in business today. To some it's become a catch-all for everything from data-gathering and synthesis to data presentation. Others see it as an actionable way to cut cost and grow revenue. It seems every day new companies sprout-up touting a level of supposed expertise on the topic that you should actually hire them to teach you! Google the phrase "analytics definition" and you get 31 million results! To help generate some level of consistency and to avoid confusion, I prefer to use this definition of analytics: "The use of relevant data that can provide insights into historical trends and lay the groundwork for a future operational framework that improves the bottom line."

THE TAKEAWAY

As you can see, analytics means different things to different people. Standardize on a definition that makes sense to you and to your organization. Take time to understand the evolving analytic capabilities of your existing business intelligence tools so that you can effectively guide your business stakeholders. Consider filling important and relevant capability gaps; however, don't let the hype around technology pull you ahead of practical, demonstrated needs. If you can't define expected and measurable business outcomes associated with an analytic capability, you probably don't need it.

INSIGHT [4]

DESCRIBING SELF-SERVICE

THE POINT: EFFECTIVE SELF-SERVICE IS A BALANCING ACT BETWEEN FREEDOM AND CONTROL

"Self-Service Analytics," writes Gartner, "is a form of business intelligence in which line-of-business professionals are enabled and encouraged to perform queries and generate reports on their own, with nominal IT support. Self-service analytics is often characterized by simple-to-use BI tools with basic analytic capabilities and an underlying data model that has been simplified or scaled down for ease of understanding and straightforward data access."[21]

Today, self-service is all the rage. Its primary focus is to empower decision-makers by enabling them to access and manipulate the data they need when they need it, to perform ad hoc queries, and to develop reports and interactive data visualizations without relying on others to do it for them. Self-service is the new model for empowering decision-makers with access to the data and technology they need to power analytics. In fact, technology is

---

[21] "Self-Service Analytics." Gartner, Inc. (http://goo.gl/Y52YF4).

advancing so fast that business users will soon find themselves with ready-access to sophisticated, advanced analytics capabilities once reserved for statisticians and quantitative analysts.

The objective is to "allow business users to wear the analyst hat."[22]—to change the way business is done by enabling decision-makers to generate actionable insight at the point of need with minimal involvement from IT.

That's important because self-service, when properly implemented, can broaden BI usage while reducing the burden on IT. Our hyper-competitive business climate continues to push resource-constrained companies to find new and innovative ways to drive client-centricity, revenue growth, and cost reduction. By pushing self-service to the enterprise, organizations can leverage the intellectual capital and untapped curiosity of its people to help drive competitive advantage.

As some point out, though, self-service is easier said than done.

"Despite its promise to liberate users from reliance on the IT department, self-service analytics is not easy to achieve," writes Wayne Eckerson, a thought leader in the business intelligence and analytics field since the early 1990s. "Many companies that have deployed self-service analytics have become inundated by a tsunami of conflicting reports, spreadmarts, renegade reporting systems, and other data silos. These companies have learned that the goal of self-service is not unfettered liberation from IT,

---

[22] TechTarget. "Self-Service BI: Major Benefits & Mistakes to Avoid." Search Business Analytics E-guide, p. 3.

but rather a partnership that balances freedom and control, flexibility and standards, governance and self-service."[23]

THE TAKEAWAY

Understand that delivering and maintaining a self-service reporting and analytics capability is hard work. It's not enough to simply democratize data and to provide business users with free-reign. To make self-service work, you need to balance end-user freedom with the right amount of centralized control.

As noted author Bernard Marr writes in a recent Forbes article, "If companies only offer self-service analytics they run the risk that people miss key insights, misinterpret the data or perform the wrong analysis. When no one is taking charge of the interpretation and analysis centrally, it often means that no one is getting the big picture."[24]

Then there's the important role IT plays in enabling and supporting self-service. Don't equate self-service with self-reliance. It's important to know what you can and cannot do on your own. Self-service can only work when business and IT work together. Take the time to recognize your organization's appetite for self-service by understanding your decision-making culture. In other words, how do your business leaders consume information and make decisions? Avoid costly data proliferation, risky data quality, and the lack of standardized processes that too often result from poorly-planned and executed self-service environments.

---

[23] Eckerson, Wayne. "A Reference Architecture for Self-Service Analytics." *KDNuggets News*. Nov. 2016. (http://goo.gl/Zm8Ubh).
[24] Marr, Bernard. "Why We Must Rethink Self-Service BI, Analytics And Reporting." *Forbes*. 25 Oct. 2016. (http://goo.gl/gaeFcp).

SECTION II
THE PEOPLE DOMAIN

INSIGHT [5]

ORGANIZATIONAL ALIGNMENT

THE POINT: ALIGNING THE BUSINESS AND IT ORGANIZATIONS IS ONE OF YOUR TOP PRIORITIES

Many companies struggle to transform information into real results. Sure, some still live in what futurist and author Thornton May calls the "analytical dark ages"[25]—where the right information is either limited or missing entirely from the organizations' decision-making processes. In my experience, though, business leaders fail to capitalize on the promise of BI because of conflicting and often divergent perspectives on what business intelligence is and how it works. What we believe influences how we behave, so, in many organizations, erroneous perceptions often lead efforts astray, they can frustrate stakeholders, and they can sap valuable budget dollars. That's why it's important for business and IT to align around fundamentals.

---

[25] May, Thornton A. *The New Know: Innovation Powered by Analytics.* Hoboken, NJ: Wiley, 2009.

It's important to know that the pressure to create value requires organizations to think differently about analytics if they want to compete and win, and that new way of thinking begins with five basic principles that help to unify stakeholders:

Unifying Principle #1 - Analytics has nothing to do with technology

Analytics is about business, not technology. Sure, technology helps make it work; but the value of any analytics initiative is ultimately driven—not by the sophistication of your visualization tools, the number of models you've deployed, or the power of your servers—but by the insight it provides and the impact it helps create. First establish your vision for analytics, then bring technology into the conversation. A capable hardware and software environment is necessary to compete on analytics. Just don't get enamored with it.

Unifying Principle #2 - Not all data matters

We live in an era of information overload. In fact, our ability to store data has outstripped our ability to use it—evidence that, even in the era of big data, more data doesn't necessarily mean more effective decision-making. Remember what Albert Einstein once said: "Not everything that counts can be counted and not everything that can be counted counts."

Unifying Principle #3 - Self-service analytics is not a project

Self-service analytics is a "business initiative," not a "technology project." Rolling out and supporting the capability is an ongoing effort to improve the organization's decision-making ability and capacity to create value. It evolves as the organization evolves. It has no finish line.

Unifying Principle #4 - Self-service isn't synonymous with "self-sufficient"

Today, many business leaders mistakenly use the idea of "self-service" to distance themselves and their teams from the people and processes that make-up IT's data management capability. These leaders correctly argue for greater speed and agility, but they take on roles and responsibilities without the requisite level of expertise or a critical enterprise perspective. In doing so, they create unacceptable risk and unnecessary cost to the organization.

In order for a firm to become an analytical competitor, the demand for and supply of data and analysis must be in alignment. Business stakeholders drive demand. They require relevant data, meaningful information, and actionable insight that enable more effective operational, tactical, and strategic decision-making. But it's the job of IT—even in a world of self-service—to source it, transform it, ensure its quality, and stage it for fast, easy access and consumption. "Supply and demand" is the place where business and IT meet. Organizations that compete on analytics rely on strong partnerships between business and IT.

Unifying Principle #5 - Attitude is everything

Our attitude doesn't just shape how others see us. It influences our actions. That makes the right attitude a prerequisite for effective collaboration and a must-have for creating the kind of cross-functional alignment you need for analytics success. Make success your passion. Dedicate yourself to exceeding your customers' expectations. Pride yourself on making your colleagues some of the best decision-makers in the world. And remember what Zig Ziglar once said: "Your attitude, not your aptitude, determines your altitude."[26]

Perspectives From The Pros

Mike Sargo
Organizational alignment is perhaps the one area where the majority of organizations consistently struggle. It's about rallying people around a vision to drive value. Those who are successful build a strong partnership between the business and information technology teams so that their respective strategies and priorities are aligned and success can be realized. The key is executive sponsorship combined with cross-functional leadership that is tasked with setting the overall vision for the program and managing its budget, governance, communication, prioritization, and change management.

Abhi Sindhwani
When it comes to implementing a successful analytics program—one that actually moves the needle in business performance—organizational alignment is of the utmost importance. Done right, it helps employees across the company understand their role in supporting the firm's overall strategy; it empowers business analysts to make required decisions; it provides a culture of accountability that incentivizes superior financial performance; and it establishes a culture of risk tolerance and trust. To be successful, though, all parts of the organization have to work in harmony.

---

[26] "Zig Ziglar Quote." *BrainyQuote*. Xplore. (http://goo.gl/Fucc2O).

THE TAKEAWAY

Organizational alignment represents one of the most overlooked aspects of creating a self-service analytics capability that really works. Don't underestimate its significance. Focus on getting business and IT aligned on the fundamentals by educating and informing them. Create a newsletter. Post articles on your intranet. Hire an industry analyst like Boris Evelson to speak at a company event. Alignment results from routine engagement and consistent messaging. Invest the time and energy necessary to build important cross-functional relationships.

INSIGHT [6]

THE ORGANIZATIONAL MODEL

THE POINT: SUPPORT YOUR DECENTRALIZED ANALYTICS TEAMS WITH A CENTRALIZED SERVICES ORGANIZATION

In my experience, the best organizational model for delivering, supporting, and effectively controlling a self-service analytics capability is what Forrester Research calls the modern, agile Business Intelligence Competency Center (BICC).[27] In short, the BICC is a hub-and-spoke structure that centralizes technology, data, and process experts in order to support decentralized business analytics professionals. According to McKinsey, these types of "hybrid organizational models often work best for broadscale analytics initiatives."[28] I agree.

Today's successful competency centers are a combination of loosely-coupled parts that often operate independently but come together, as needed, to form a virtual, shared-services

---

[27] Evelson, Boris. "Agile Business Intelligence Solution Centers Are More Than Just Competency Centers." *Build An Insights-Driven Org Blog.* Forrester Research, Inc. 6 Jun. 2018. (http://goo.gl/EJFJCP).

[28] Fleming, Oliver, Tim Fountaine, Nicolaus Henke, and Tamim Saleh. "Ten red flags signaling your analytics program will fail." McKinsey & Company. Jun. 2018. (http://goo.gl/Z2L8Ju).

51

organization. This model ensures the kind of responsiveness and scalability required for success without having to prematurely or unnecessarily invest in dedicated human capital.

A competency center is a service and delivery organization to the business. Its primary mission is to engage, enable, and empower. For some, that means how to best implement and use the right platforms and tools, how to ensure ready-access to comprehensive and trustworthy data, or how to create standard analytic methods that are properly governed. For others, the center's mandate is to focus on training and development, documenting and socializing best practices, or fostering an environment of collaboration and shared intellectual capital. Perhaps, for you and your organization, it's a combination of all of the above.

I'm often asked, "Where should a competency center live?" In other words, "Who owns it?" To answer that question, there are two things you need to understand. First, it's important that a competency center maintains an enterprise perspective. That means it's neither IT-centric nor project-based. Second, to do its job well, the competency center needs the ability to influence data strategy, architecture, governance, and a myriad of other data- and process-related items.

In my experience, a competency center can best satisfy these two critical success factors by being an integral part of IT where is has visibility into enterprise priorities and funding and where it can build and influence a broad array of relationships necessary to achieve its advocacy role for the business.

THE TAKEAWAY

Unlike a traditional center of excellence that focuses almost exclusively on strategy and best practices—the "what," a competency center's primary role is to get things done—the "how." Strategy and planning are important but only to the extent that they inform the delivery of real results. As Forrester points out, someone has to actually roll-up his sleeves and work in the trenches to architect, design, develop, test, implement, and support the firm's analytics initiatives and associated applications.[29] That's the role of a competency center. Remember that self-service functions, by definition, through decentralized analytics teams. It's the centralized services organization that makes the model work by knocking down departmental silos, fostering collaboration, and ensuring line of business analysts are adequately supported to do their jobs.

[29] Ibid.

INSIGHT [7]

THE IMPORTANCE OF COLLABORATION

THE POINT: ELIMINATE DEPARTMENTAL SILOS

To borrow a phrase from Adam Richardson, Assistant VP of Strategy and Marketing at global innovation firm Frog Design, "Collaboration is a team sport."[30] You wouldn't know that stepping inside the operation of most firms where departmental silos rule. It's easier for most folks, I suppose, to shield themselves from the inconvenience and hard work that often accompanies collaboration and, instead, focus on getting their own work done. But, believe it or not, organizations rely on collaboration to increase business value. That's because collaboration impacts productivity, quality, innovation, customer service, and financial performance. "As a general rule, global companies that collaborate better, perform better," says Dr. Jaclyn Kostner, best-selling author of the book, *Virtual*

---

[30] Richardson, Adam. "Collaboration Is a Team Sport, and You Need to Warm Up." *Harvard Business Review*. 31 May 2011. (http://goo.gl/xouuvL).

Leadership. "Those that collaborate less, do not perform as well. It's just that simple."[31]

"The problem," writes author and Forbes contributor Bernard Marr, "is that the people being given access to the data aren't analysts, and don't necessarily have the mindset or skillset to view the data holistically." He believes that organizations that offer self-service only, without some level of centralized control, run the risk of misinterpreting data and missing key insights. "When no one is taking charge of the interpretation and analysis centrally," say Marr, "it often means that no one is getting the big picture."[32]

That's why collaboration is so important. Self-service silos pose obvious issues, like duplication of effort, risk from non-standardized processes, and data proliferation. But, as Forrester Research points out, "moving too far in the other direction toward a fully centralized, shared-services BI organization often creates rigidity and bureaucratic layers of control."[33] Organizations must make a concerted effort to break-down the departmental silos that prevent effective collaboration and enable the sharing of intellectual capital, standardized analytic processes, and best practices so important to self-service success. After all, as Ken Blanchard so aptly puts it in *The One Minute Manager®*, "None of us is as smart as all of us."

---

[31] "Chapter 2: Global E-business .and Collaboration." (http://goo.gl/88OUvb).

[32] Marr, Bernard. "Why We Must Rethink Self-Service BI, Analytics And Reporting." *Forbes.* 25 Oct. 2016. (http://goo.gl/hp5YZ5).

[33] Evelson, Boris. "Agile Business Intelligence Solution Centers Are More Than Just Competency Centers."

PERSPECTIVES FROM THE PROS

Mike Sargo

Collaboration and communication across disparate business units of any organization can be transformational to decision-making, but it can also be an impossible challenge when leaders focus primarily on the success of their particular business units without regard to the greater good of the organization. To be successful with business intelligence, organizations have to break down departmental silos, share information across the enterprise, and collaborate with one another.

Abhi Sindhwani

Collaboration is essential for business and should be an integral part of any analytics effort. It's not that collaboration is all that difficult, either. It's just that varying priorities often pull employees in different directions. When an enterprise collaborates around analytics, it minimizes redundant, costly, and counterproductive efforts while maximizing the visibility required to drive results. All it takes is a commitment to transparency, a desire to communicate, and a willingness to keep the big picture in mind.

THE TAKEAWAY

The synergistic power of the group can be a real competitive differentiator, so work hard to break down departmental silos that keep people from talking and sharing. Effective collaboration can help leverage the intellectual capital that exists across the enterprise and ensure your analytics capability is always aligned with business need.

INSIGHT [8]

THE RIGHT TEAM

THE POINT: BE YOUR COMPANY'S BATMAN

While you need to get your organizational model right and understand the important role collaboration plays in long-term success, the team itself will ultimately determine how you compete and if you win. I'm not talking about how smart or sophisticated people are, whether they have advanced degrees in analytics, or even how well they communicate in their roles. Though, as McKinsey points out, "Organizations [do] need a variety of analytics talent with well-defined roles" to be successful with business intelligence.[34] In my opinion, the right team is the team with the right mindset.

In *Thinking for a Change*, author John Maxwell writes about big-picture thinking, focused thinking, creative thinking, and shared thinking. "Good thinkers," he writes, "are never at a loss to solve problems. They never lack ideas that can help to build an organization."[35]

---

[34] Fleming. "Ten red flags signaling your analytics program will fail."
[35] Maxwell, John C. *Thinking for a Change*. Boston, Mass.: Center Street, 2005.

These are the folks I call business superheroes: ordinary individuals with extraordinary attitudes. They have a passion for the possible and an unrelenting will to do transformative work. They also share ten characteristics in common:[36]

1. **They never give up.** Business superheroes overcome challenges by wholeheartedly committing themselves to unrelenting persistence.

2. **They always get the job done.** There are no excuses. You either save the day or you don't.

3. **Superheroes are the best at what they do.** They excel in areas where their superpowers are needed most.

4. **Business superheroes are crystal clear in their purpose.** They are always focused and results-oriented.

5. **They recognize their flaws.** The goal in anything they do is never perfection. It's the pursuit of perfection.

6. **Superheroes don't seek glory.** They do what they do because it's the right thing to do.

7. **They help others.** Superheroes are never obsessed with themselves but with helping other people solve problems.

8. **Business superheroes enjoy teamwork.** They know they are more powerful when they are part of a team of

---

[36] Adapted from "10 Traits Entrepreneurs Share With Superheroes." Startup America Partnership. 21 Mar. 2015. (http://goo.gl/tLYSPC).

superheroes. When you're taking on the world, help is vital.

9. **They know that true strength comes from their character.** Superheroes are always courageous, respectful, honorable, and selfless.

10. **Superheroes accomplish great feats.** They're effective at what they do because they keep their eyes on the prize.

We often relate the concept of a superhero to our favorite cartoon character or some masked avenger who uses superhuman power to fight crime on the streets of a big city. The business superhero isn't that kind of guy. He's more like Batman—described by comic book artist Neal Adams as the only superhero who isn't really a superhero at all. "He has no powers," writes Adams. "He's [simply] a human being bent on a mission."[37]

Be your company's Batman.

PERSPECTIVES FROM THE PROS

Mike Sargo

Dysfunction kills teamwork and wastes valuable time and money. So, the right team is a team without dysfunction—if such a thing exists. Dysfunction manifests itself in a variety of ways including team members who miss meetings or deliverables because "something came up"; poor communication; a lack of transparency; whispered discontent; second-guessing; finger-

---

[37] Zehr, E. Paul. *Becoming Batman: The Possibility of a Superhero*. The Johns Hopkins University Press, 2008.

pointing. You know it when you see it. The key is to address it right away.

Sri Seepana

Our industry is evolving so rapidly that it's critical for analytics teams to keep pace. To me, the right team is a team that has the means, desire, and mandate to evolve its capabilities around emerging technologies and to align those capabilities with business value in order to maximize effectiveness. People have to be flexible enough to change when the business demands it.

Abhi Sindhwani

When I think of a team, I think of a group of individuals who come together to form a cohesive unit focused on the work of transformation. So, the "right team" is a team that not just thinks the right way but acts the right way, too. Every member has a specific personal role to play, and the role is both defined and understood. The team, though, works for the good of the goal. To align and focus the right team, a colleague of mine uses a framework similar to Bruce Tuckman's forming-storming-norming-performing model of group development. She calls it absorb-accept-advance, and we use it to drive effective teamwork that helps to propel our analytics agenda forward by ensuring everyone is aligned. If your team isn't aligned, you don't have the right team.

THE TAKEAWAY

Successful people think differently than unsuccessful people. They have the right mindset. They are outside-the-box thinkers who approach new ideas by saying "yes, if" rather than "no, because." They see the big-picture. They are focused and creative. Ian Gordon, a member of the editorial review team for this book, offered me a great observation about superheroes. "Superheroes," he said, "are actually the people who make sure you don't need [literal] superheroes to react and fix things." I couldn't agree more. To me, Mr. Gordon describes the ordinary guy or gal with the extraordinary attitude—someone who is simply bent on a mission. The fixers are the ones who are often lauded; however, as Mr. Gordon points out, the ones who ensure we don't need fixers are the true superheroes.

INSIGHT [9]

THE RIGHT SUPPORT

THE POINT: SELF-SERVICE ANALYTICS REQUIRES AN EDUCATED, INFORMED, AND SUPPORTED USER COMMUNITY

If you want to make self-service analytics work, you need to know your users. Your user community is diverse, and maturity varies when it comes to business acumen, analytic prowess, and technical capability. In order to empower them, you need to bridge-the-gap with the right education, training, and awareness programs.

Nearly every business defines its user community differently. In Figure 9-1, I use The Analytics Journey from Insight 3 to map three typical user types to their analytics activity.

Casual users (often referred to as information "consumers") represent the vast majority of business intelligence users across your enterprise—perhaps up to 85% or more. They might be tellers in the branch of a bank, retail store managers, or quality control specialists on a shop floor. They aren't analysts, but they need information to monitor and measure the work they do. They

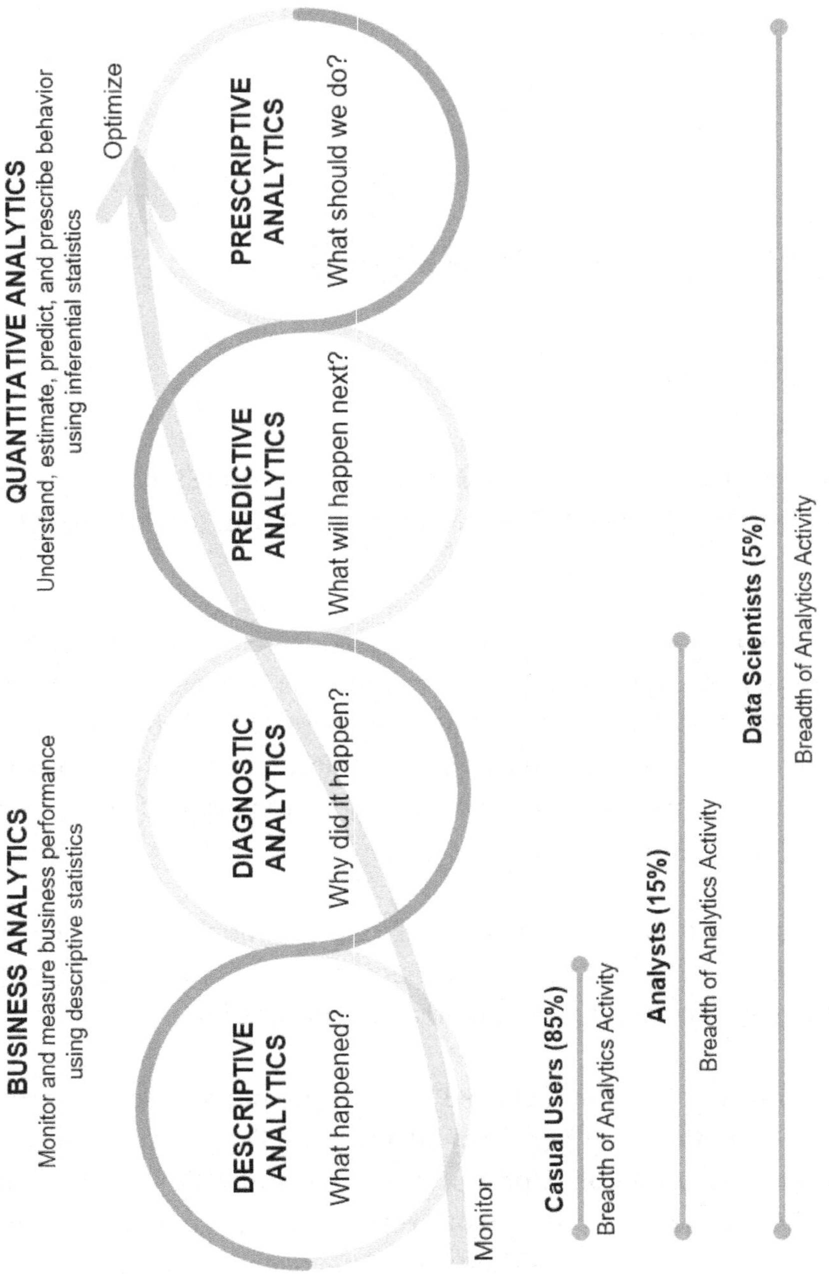

Figure 9.1 – User Classifications

focus primarily on descriptive analytics and typically consume information provided to them by others. This represents the breadth of their activity.

Analysts, a much smaller group within your user community, are your power users. I refer to them as your analytics creators. They are the investigators and explorers who focus a lot of time on descriptive and diagnostic analytics to help establish and support business strategy and execution. Analysts are line of business subject matter experts who know how to access, prepare, and interpret data necessary to run the business.

Data scientists are analytics specialists. Most companies have only a handful—5% or less of your total user community—but these "inventors" solve complex business problems using the most advanced technology, analytics techniques, and data available. Their expertise enables organizations to create new and innovative ways of servicing customers, generating revenue, and managing risk. Data scientists use whatever type of analytics is necessary to meet their needs, so their work spans the entire analytics journey.

Figure 9-2 provides general profile information for each user type. Notice that support requirements vary.

USER TYPE	BUSINESS KNOWLEDGE	ANALYTICAL SKILLS	EXAMPLE TECHNOLOGIES	SUPPORT REQUIRED
Casual Users (Consumers)	Basic	Basic Simple reports, dashboards, and visualizations	Operational Systems, IBM Cognos, Salesforce, Tableau	Data literacy Technology orientation Technical support
Analysts	Intermediate to Advanced	Intermediate Statistical, comparative, and root cause analysis; scenario modeling; data visualization	Tableau, SAS, SQL, Alteryx, Excel	Training and technical support Data literacy Data storytelling
Data Scientists	Advanced	Advanced Inferential statistics; data visualization; modeling; machine learning; data mining	SAS, R, Python, Pandas, Scala, MatLab, Java, Jupyter, Spark, MongoDB	Training and certification Technology advancements Data literacy

Figure 9-2 - User Type Profile

The point is to profile your user community so that you understand who they are, the skills they have, and the jobs they need to perform. You'll then be in good position to determine the right type and level of support.

Be creative, though. Support programs can take many forms and should align with the learning styles of your user community. For example, I like to offer technology "orientation" sessions. Unlike formal training which is often all-encompassing, orientation focuses on the "how to" of functionality folks need to know. Coupled with presentation materials and cheat sheets, orientation is perfect for busy professionals who just have to get their jobs done. Orientation sessions also avoid the "use it or lose it" problem associated with formal training.

When it comes to support, I'm also big on data literacy.

One aspect of data literacy deals with the five characteristics of good data. I cover this in Section V. But good data is only relevant if it's easily accessible and understood. Your self-service analytics community needs to know where to find data, what the data means, who owns it, how to access it, and what restrictions exist around its use. Consider an internal data marketplace to solve this problem.

Along with self-service analytics comes the idea of self-service support, so build, deploy, and maintain a user-searchable knowledgebase for self-help. But don't reinvent the wheel. Use the proven community support frameworks already deployed by many of the leading BI vendors as a guide to what works.

Other support ideas that work include lunch and learn sessions, internal webinars, "art of the possible" sessions that introduce new technology, internal "how to" reference videos, best practice guidelines and templates, and "the doctor is in" sessions that provide one-on-one consultative help.

PERSPECTIVES FROM THE PROS

Sri Seepana

The proportion of enterprise users touched by self-service continues to expand, and that means effective support is growing increasingly important. The challenge is that analytics needs differ across the enterprise, so it's imperative that you understand the users that make-up your analytics community. It's not enough to know what your users do or the departments in which they work. Evaluate their background, technical knowledge, and level of business acumen, too. And be sure to consider their long-term needs, not just the short-term ones.

Abhi Sindhwani

Establishing user expectations around support should be at the core of any self-service analytics initiative. It's not difficult. Just ask. Then ask "why?" to gain a deeper understanding of the real need and the drivers behind it. Broadly communicate what you learn, and solicit feedback so you can identify and address any questions, concerns, or misunderstandings. Once you align expectations and implement the support program, check-in with users on a routine basis to ensure everything is working as planned. By making users an integral part of the process, they feel valued and heard. You build advocates as a result.

THE TAKEAWAY

No organization is successful when its people work in silos. A well-supported user community is an empowered user community. Be service-oriented, and put processes in place to address the pressing support needs of the business. Analytics users need to focus on the creation of value, not how to use a tool or where to find data.

SECTION III
THE PROCESS DOMAIN

INSIGHT [10]

SETTING PRIORITIES

THE POINT: FOCUS ON THINGS THAT MATTER

In today's business climate, it's easy to get distracted. So how do successful business leaders set priorities amidst a never-ending stream of pressing matters that compete for time, attention, and precious financial resources? They identify and focus on things that make a difference. In their book, *The Art of Transfomation*, authors Gingrich and Desmond compare the business leader's need to focus with the focus some animals demonstrate in the wild. "They're like lions," the authors write. "Lions have to distinguish between antelopes and chipmunks. If they focus on the wrong thing, they'll starve to death."[38] Decision-makers face the same harsh reality in the world of business.

Your ability to use self-service analytics to generate insight that is relevant, timely, and actionable requires a fundamental understanding of the key strategic, tactical, and operational questions that occupy your organization's decision-makers. I

---

[38] Gingrich, Newt, and Nancy Desmond. *The Art of Transformation*. CHT Press, 2006.

refer to these questions as "mission critical"—they are typically the first questions leaders ask when they arrive at work in the morning and the last things they think about when they leave at the end of the day. Let me frame it another way: How would you respond if I asked you to tell me the one question you better be able to answer in order to keep your job? That's a mission-critical question. See, when a business leader is unable to answer a mission-critical question, he's enduring "business pain." For business and IT practitioners tasked with building and growing a self-service capability, the identification and elimination of this pain is a top priority.

In its report on the evolution of business intelligence, predictive analytics firm Prevedere quotes Gartner research that indicates between 70% to 80% of corporate business intelligence projects fail to deliver the insight business needs. Report authors go on to say that only one-third of CEOs trust the accuracy of internal analytics, according to a study by KPMG.[39]

These CEOs and the organizations they run are starving to death. Set your priorities by focusing on things that matter.

PERSPECTIVES FROM THE PROS

Mike Sargo
Priority-setting is one of the more critical aspect to building a successful analytics program. It involves choosing which projects the organization should commit its valuable resources to amidst a multitude of competing initiatives. This isn't a "one

---

[39] "The Evolution of Business Intelligence Report." Prevedere, 2018. (http://goo.gl/dqmeYP).

and done" effort either. Priorities have to change out of necessity as the business changes. The business intelligence team should work closely with the business users as part of the process to make sure there is both strong alignment to business strategy and buy-in from stakeholders. I've seen countless technical teams decide they know what's best or assume they know what business users want only to miss the mark when delivering. No organization can afford this critical mistake. Consistent collaboration is the only real way to deliver results that count. When evaluating potential use cases, consider strategic alignment, expected value, and project complexity. A quick rating against these three dimensions will help you weed out projects that really don't make sense.

Sri Seepana

In my opinion, expected business value should always be the primary factor when prioritizing self-service analytics projects. Now, it's important to recognize that the definition of value could change from time to time depending on business direction and market conditions. Such a change could demand a change in priorities, too. However, expected Return On Investment (ROI) should be the one consistent, measurable metric the business uses to prioritize access to limited financial resources and analytics talent.

Abhi Sindhwani

Every organization struggles with setting priorities, especially when it comes to analytics. Some firms give highest priority to use cases that support operations. Others like to focus on innovation and R&D. Many give the highest priority to efforts that boost the financial bottom line. I think trying to establish a universal standard is a waste of time. The prioritization framework I've used with a lot of success is simple and straightforward because it focuses, first and foremost, on the ongoing viability of the organization. I describe them this way:

Priority 1 - Lights On, Doors Open (LODO)
Priority 2 - Improve/Boost Financials
Priority 3 - Innovation/Research and Development

THE TAKEAWAY

While those of us who design, build, and deploy analytics solutions like to believe there is no greater investment priority for the business, this isn't always the case. In fact, there is always demand for an organization's limited people and financial resources. Set priorities based on a model that works the way your company works. McKinsey suggests that analytics use cases be prioritized based on feasibility and impact.[40] Other things to consider are your organization's decision-making culture; its appetite for risk; the availability of data with adequate breadth, depth, and quality; the effort's level of expected disruption; and the speed at which you can execute. Once you have a framework for prioritization in place, work hard to validate and tune it based on the outcomes.

---

[40] Fleming.

INSIGHT [11]

BALANCING RISK AND REWARD

THE POINT: KEEP THINGS SIMPLE

Complexity is wreaking havoc on business. One study conducted by the Warwick Business School looked at the world's two hundred largest companies and found they were wasting over a billion dollars a year resulting from, among other things, overly complex business processes.[41]

Organizations unwittingly overcomplicate analytics, too. Avoidable complexity often arises from poor communication between business and IT, from practitioners trying to do way too much (and taking way too long in the process), from analytics teams over-architecting solutions, and from project leaders micromanaging the effort. Self-service analytics works best when the process of moving from great idea to actionable insight is fast and focused.

---

[41] Siegel, Alan. *Simple: Conquering the Crisis of Complexity.* S.l.: Grand Central, 2013.

"Simple is smart," write Alan Siegel and Irene Etzkorn, authors of *Simple: Conquering the Crisis of Complexity*.[42] In fact, here are a few simple things you can do to effectively balance risk and reward:

Keep It Simple Rule #1 - Focus on business enablement

The speed of business is only increasing. So, when it comes to providing decision-makers with the information they need to do their jobs, rapid time-to-results is absolutely critical. Firms need to adapt their analytics design-build-deploy process, technology infrastructures, and governance frameworks so that they strike the right balance between maintaining control and enabling the business to get on with its job. Create an environment that enables you to respond quickly to business needs. Build and deliver according to lightweight standards established by I.T, then integrate the new capability into your enterprise environment following a pre-determined, agreed-upon process.

Keep It Simple Rule #2 - Crawl, walk, run

One of the best approaches for securing executive buy-in to analytics initiatives is the concept of incremental development; that is, building or expanding your reporting and analytic capability over time, one step at a time. Executives embrace this approach for a couple of good reasons: 1.) it helps to minimize exposure and risk; and 2.) it enables business leaders to use "demonstrated value" as justification for continued investment. You can't boil the ocean, so don't overcomplicate your analytics effort by taking on so much that you fail to deliver quickly. Crawl, walk, run is about dividing and conquering—simplifying an otherwise complex process in order to show valuable, incremental progress.

---

[42] Ibid.

Keep It Simple Rule #3 - Start with existing technology

Most organizations have already made significant investments in business intelligence tools and related infrastructure including the development of intellectual capital that only comes with experience and time. When building and growing your analytics capability, always start with existing technology. Prove that it can't or won't work before requesting additional funds.

THE TAKEAWAY

The key to balancing risk and reward is to keep things simple. Don't get caught-up in the complexities of people, processes, technology, or data. Instead, focus your energy on identifying high-value, low-risk opportunities to eliminate business pain, and then execute with speed and agility in a crawl, walk, run fashion. Work overtime to bridge the communication, trust, and understanding gap that represents today's business-IT relationship. And always remember what British economist E.F. Schumacher once said: "Any intelligent fool can make things bigger more complex.... It takes a touch of genius—and a lot of courage—to move in the opposite direction."[43]

---

[43] "E. F. Schumacher Quote." *BrainyQuote*. Xplore. (http://goo.gl/HAPLfE).

INSIGHT [12]

BUILDING REQUIREMENTS THAT WORK

THE POINT: AVOID THE PROBLEM OF POOR REQUIREMENTS BY CHANGING YOUR APPROACH

Truth be told, creating requirements for analytics solutions is tough business. Few decision-makers really know what information they need to do their jobs, and pressure to drive performance in a constantly-changing business environment can make requirements difficult to button-down. To make matters worse, most of the techniques used to gather requirements today are still systems- and software-oriented, and they are simply inadequate in delivering on the promise of BI with the kind of speed and responsiveness required by today's business leaders. More than a decade ago BusinessWeek Research Services ranked poor requirements among the top obstacles to avoid if you wanted to be successful with BI.[44] That finding still holds true today.

---

[44] "Getting Smart About BI: Best Practices Deliver Real Value." *BusinessWeek Research Services*, Sep. 2006. (http://goo.gl/rSUdWR).

In order to avoid the problem of poor requirements, you need to change your approach to gathering them. In my book, Hyper, I present an 8-step accelerated approach to creating, validating, and communicating requirements that I call the Quick Wins Model. Its purpose is to help you deliver a comprehensive, business-aligned analytics capability over time, one fast-paced step at a time.

Whether you use the Quick Wins Model or not, you need to keep some guiding principles in mind as you think about building requirements that work.

Requirements Principle #1 - Know your organization

One of the keys to maximizing the effectiveness of your requirements-gathering effort is to ensure you have a strong, foundational understanding of how your organization makes decisions—and who makes them. Take time to brief yourself on your firm's strategies and corporate initiatives, objectives, and departmental plans so that you can effectively guide stakeholder discussions.

Requirements Principle #2 - Think front of mind

When building a self-service analytics capability that is responsive to the needs of the business, you are only interested in requirements that are "front of mind." It's this level of stakeholder awareness that drives the identification of quick wins. Forget about everything else.

Requirements Principle #3 - Expectations matter

Most of the time, getting a business user's point of view on important topics like big plans, critical success factors, barriers to success, and constraints is something that is either neglected entirely during traditional requirements-gathering exercises or simply overshadowed by a preoccupation with functional specifications. It's a mistake you don't want to make with self-service analytics. That's because understanding and effectively managing stakeholder expectations has a direct, significant, and lasting impact on solution adoption. Adoption is "personal buy-in"— a user's response to feeling involved, heard, and understood. At the end of the day, the level of adoption represents a real and practical way stakeholders tell us that their analytics capability is in or out of alignment with their needs.

PERSPECTIVES FROM THE PROS

Sri Seepana

Complex business problems often have complex analytics requirements that need translated into simple solutions. To do that, you need to define requirements and execute on them in digestible chunks. Speed and agility are the new norm, and that makes the idea of failing fast so important. Aim to deliver in small incremental steps so that requirements can be adjusted and your solution tuned as business needs dictate. Focus on effective collaboration to ensure alignment between business and IT, and be mindful of transparency in all communication.

THE TAKEAWAY

Requirements are a critical foundation in building a self-service analytics capability. They can make or break your effort. The approach you take to gathering them and the speed at which you execute on them will ultimately determine how successful you are.

INSIGHT [13]

EVALUATE AND EVOLVE

THE POINT: ROUTINELY EVALUATE AND EVOLVE YOUR SELF-SERVICE CAPABILITY TO ENSURE CONTINUED SUCCESS

Building a competency in self-service analytics is an evolutionary process. It's one of the reasons I created the Quick Wins Model that I reference in Insight 12. It helps guide you through quick iterations of planning and execution cycles so that you have the opportunity to "fail fast." Failing fast is important because real learning happens and real insight results from trial and error.

In their book, *The Wisdom of Failure: How to Learn the Tough Leadership Lessons Without Paying the Price*, authors Larry Weinzimmer and Jim McConoughey talk about the importance of failure on the road to success. "Failure is the only option," they write, "if success is the end goal."[45] That's hard to hear if you work for one of the many organizations that have invested significant time, energy, and financial resources in BI and still

---

[45] Weinzimmer, Larry and Jim McConoughey. "Failure Is The Only Option If Success Is The End Goal." *Fast Company*. 7 Sep. 2012. (http://goo.gl/8sWn8B).

struggle to see success. McKinsey agrees. "It is surprising how many companies are spending millions of dollars on advanced analytics and other digital investments but are unable to attribute any bottom-line impact to these investments."[46]

Sure, some deployments work and generate measurable results. But BI adoption remains flat, and the majority of initiatives still report only slight to moderate success and business impact. Unfortunately, organizations forget that business intelligence is a journey—a process of continuous improvement meant to adapt and evolve. Too many practitioners build and deliver a capability but then think the work is done. They don't take the time to qualify success—to proactively monitor and measure BI performance against expectation.

There are two important "monitoring" questions you need to ask yourself in order to effectively evaluate and evolve self-service:

1. **Are the analytics capabilities and actionable insight that I'm providing helping to generate the business outcomes my stakeholders expect when they expect them?**

   Enhance those areas that are "on target" so you can drive even greater value. For those that are missing the mark, analyze why and then adjust accordingly. Remember that analytics success "doesn't just happen." It is a process of continuous improvement

2. **Is my technology environment high-performing?**

   The same holds true for your physical environment. "BI performance efficiency and effectiveness metrics play a

---

46 Fleming.

key role in helping to improve the efficacy of the BI environment. Companies that track these metrics can contextualize BI usage patterns and trends to predict requests from users before they even make them."[47] Forrester Research calls this "BI on BI" and has established a body-of knowledge on the subject.

Interestingly enough, Forrester estimates that only about half of BI pros take the time to quantitatively measure the effectiveness or efficiency of the environments they manage. Put yourself in the right half. Just remember that creating a responsive analytics environment is an evolutionary process, too; but you can't improve what you don't measure.

PERSPECTIVES FROM THE PROS

Mike Sargo

To me, business intelligence programs should be in a constant state of evolution. After all, analytics requirements change just as businesses change. It's critical they stay aligned. Alignment, though, requires routine evaluation of expected business outcomes and a re-evaluation of priorities. I've worked with a number of organizations that worked very hard in the early stages of their analytics initiatives to set a good vision and a strong roadmap; however, they ultimately failed because they never took a step back to evaluate their work or to consider any deviations from initial plans. They became so focused on the

---

[47] Bennett, Martha, Boris Evelson, Holger Kisker, and Carmen Stoica. "BI on BI: How To Manage The Performance of BI Initiatives." Forrester Research, Inc. 22 Dec. 2014. (http://goo.gl/mtGIFFN).

initial objectives that they never considered how the business might change in the process. Change happens: new systems get deployed; regulations evolve; acquisitions occur; people leave. To hit the mark with analytics, you need to embrace change and be mindful of the need for routine evaluation.

Sri Seepana

One thing you need in place to monitor and measure success is an analytics roadmap. Its creation is the way you get business unit leaders aligned around the organization's strategic vision for self-service, the prioritization of tactical projects, and the definition of success. The roadmap, then, is critical for establishing performance and outcome expectations upon which the organization's self-service capability is evaluated.

THE TAKEAWAY

Continuous improvement is a key success factor in a healthy self-service world. Put the right plans in place to align the organization so that everyone moves in the same direction. Then embrace change as an important influencing factor as you work to evolve your capability.

INSIGHT [14]

SELL THE VISION

THE POINT: AN ENGAGED AND MOTIVATED USER COMMUNITY CAN TRANSFORM AN ORGANIZATION

It's been my experience that skeptics and naysayers fill the ranks of most organizations. You know them. They like the status quo. They resist change. They make comments like "we've been down this road before" and "I'll believe it when I see it." At best, they are tough-minded "demanders of proof" willing to believe if you only show them the way. At worst, they are obstructionists who can unwittingly prevent your analytics initiative from yielding expected returns.

Creating an insights-driven culture built on self-service analytics requires a lot of things I cover in this book. One of the most important is vision. You need to sell the dream—to build a sustainable level of momentum and excitement that captures the hearts and minds of your stakeholders. That's because an engaged and motivated user community can literally transform your organization.

Consider yourself a business-oriented technology evangelist. Your job is to socialize, market, and sell a vision for and the resulting benefits of self-service analytics. The purpose is to educate, inform, and motivate your audience into a critical mass of support that helps drive adoption and long-term sustainability. Your job is to amplify—to raise your voice and be heard. Let me give you some tips for making it happen:

Amplify Tip #1 - Create an identity

When you create an identity for your analytics initiative, you empower yourself to internally market and sell in ways that engage your audience. Think contests, events, posters, banners, T-shirts, mugs, laptop stickers, and a host of other options. And don't just name your initiative, brand it. "When you think about [a] brand," says Forbes contributing writer Lois Gellar, "think about all the elements [that make it up]: promise, personality, look, voice, service, attributes, memorability, even [impression]."[48] A brand sets expectations around value and gives your stakeholders something to hold onto. Hey, if you want a best-in-class analytics capability, act best-in-class.

Amplify Tip #2 - Establish advocates

Not everyone is a skeptic. In fact, you'd never be able to staff the right team I talk about in Insight 8 if that were the case. So, dedicate time to identifying advocates—those business and IT practitioners who "get self-service analytics" and your vision for the future. They can act as important surrogates in their circles of influence. Build rapport and invite them into your inner circle. Advocates are a great way to informally educate, to casually inform, and to spread key messages that are

---

48 Geller, Lois. "Why A Brand Matters." *Forbes*. 23 May 2012. (http://goo.gl/ZCt66T).

necessary for building the enterprise support you need for long-term success.

Amplify Tip #3 - Promote your successes

Nothing generates more buzz or builds more momentum than a great story. Analytics is all about storytelling, so promote the delivery of every win, and make sure your entire organization hears about the success stories from sales, marketing, finance, and operations that result from the use of self-service analytics. Excited people talk, so get people excited!

Amplify Tip #4 - Communicate often

Education and transparency are good things. So, think of simple and easy ways to routinely "over-communicate" key messages, status updates, project countdowns, and other information of interest to your audience. Use a newsletter, an intranet page, or strategically-placed posters. Give business unit leaders weekly talking points they can deliver during staff meetings. Or get creative and produce a series of podcasts or web videos. You can even interview decision-makers from the set of your very own virtual studio.

Amplify Tip #5 - Be prepared for questions and feedback

Once you open-up broad-based communication with your audience, expect a lot of questions and considerable feedback. Consider it a prime opportunity to deepen the level of engagement. Be responsive and appreciative. In fact, consider publishing a running Q&A in your newsletter or highlighting feedback in your podcast to promote free-flowing discussion and idea generation.

PERSPECTIVES FROM THE PROS

Mike Sargo

There are two techniques I use to socialize, market, and sell the value of self-service analytics. Both I've found effective depending on the culture and analytics maturity of the organization. The first is the POC. A proof-of-concept is a great way to create dialogue, to drive understanding, and to gain early support. People love a "show and tell," especially when it centers around a high-value business problem that isn't easily solved through traditional BI. The second technique is an analytics roadshow. Typically targeted at line of business leaders, the purpose of the roadshow is to demonstrate analytics capabilities, discuss the art of the possible, and interact around the LOB's high-value user cases. Both techniques enable you create important relationships and to embed the right kind of messaging in your presentation material.

Sri Seepana

Selling the vision isn't about pushing a self-service analytics agenda and working to convince people to follow it. Rather, it's a natural outcome when business and IT effectively partner and collaborate. The internal marketability of an analytics effort relies upon opportunity identification, a compelling value proposition, and a demonstration that the organization can deliver—usually in the form of a proof-of-concept. Altogether, these factors help to motivate and inspire.

THE TAKEAWAY

Left unattended, the culture of most organizations will marginalize a BI initiative to the point of limited (and unacceptable) return. In fact, I believe culture-related issues are a primary cause of the stagnate adoption and lackluster performance we've seen from business intelligence efforts over the past decade. That's why it's so important to establish a plan to internally socialize, market, and sell. Did you know that in 2016-2017, MindBody, Salesforce, Bottomline Technologies, Tableau, Oracle and Johnson & Johnson all had marketing and sales budgets that were greater than 20% of revenue, some spending close to 50%![49] "Determining the effect of marketing on a company's growth is not black and white," writes Sara Brady, a digital marketing content manager for creative agency Vital. "There are many factors that combine to create a successful and growing business. However, without marketing a company gets very little, if any, promotion or exposure, meaning the chances of growth are slim to none."[50] Don't underestimate marketing's power to educate, influence, and persuade your stakeholders—to help build and grow a self-service analytics culture in your company.

---

[49] Brady, Sarah. "What Percent of Revenue Do Publicly Traded Companies Spend on Marketing and Sales?" *Vital*. 11 Jun. 2018. (http://goo.gl/GkWFDB).
[50] Ibid.

INSIGHT [15]

CONTROL THE CHAOS

THE POINT: ANARCHY CAN PARALYZE AN ORGANIZATION

Left uncontrolled, self-service analytics can quickly turn into anarchy. You need to manage and control it, and the key is to use lightweight governance that's business-led and process-driven. Sure, business users want self-service that is both agile and flexible, but most recognize the importance of governance. In fact, they want assurance that the data they are going after can be trusted, access is there when they need it, and that their system is high-performing. After all, they have a job to do.

Organizations without a governance strategy? Well, they've paid the price. "Business units gradually produce spreadmarts and reporting shadow systems that undermine the data consistency required to align an organization," writes Wayne Eckerson. The noted speaker and consultant goes on to say that, "In the worst case—which is almost every client I work with—self-service BI creates an environment in which no one trusts the data that anyone else produces. [And] because everyone creates reports using their own data and calculates metrics uniquely, there is widespread distrust of the data. Self-service creates a proverbial

Tower of Babel where everyone is empowered with data but no one can communicate."[51]

In order to control the chaos, though, you first need to understand the distinction between "data governance" and the business-oriented, process-driven governance I'm talking about called "BI governance."

Data governance aligns the right people, processes, and technology required to integrate, secure, optimize, and utilize an organization's enterprise information assets. It is all encompassing and includes master data management, metadata management, data quality, and data stewardship. Data governance is notoriously complex and rigid because its primary focus is the hardening of data assets that support a myriad of enterprise use cases, not just business intelligence.

On the other hand, BI governance only deals with who consumes data, when, how, and for what reporting or analytics purposes. Forrester defines BI governance as "a combination of policies, processes, and technologies that allow business and technology pros to collaborate, manage, monitor, and adjust BI usage to maximize BI value and effectiveness."[52] BI governance helps to inform data governance policies and analytics best practices.

The concept of BI governance is well-suited to the pace and agility required to make self-service analytics work. Rather than it being a standalone initiative, BI governance is an essential part of every analytics workstream. That way it empowers your users

---

[51] Eckerson, Wayne. "Governed Data Discovery: Blending Self-Service and Standards.' *Upside*. 28 Jul. 2016. (http://goo.gl/jXmo3y).

[52] Evelson, Boris. "Divide (BI Governance From Data Governance) And Conquer."

while effectively supporting the incremental development of your self-service capability.

Forrester's approach to BI governance is based on a five-step process:[53]

BI Governance Step #1 - Monitor

BI is no different from any other business process: the monitor step forms the basis for all other steps in the BI governance process, since you cannot effectively govern without actionable insights. Forrester calls this process BI on BI.[54] It's the starting point for profiling your user community—understanding who is doing what with data, when, and how often.

BI Governance Step #2 - Inform

Knowledge is a major contributor to BI governance success. BI on BI does part of the trick, but knowing where data originates for reporting and analytics and what it looks like is a key success factor. This step focuses on data lineage analysis, data profiling, and understanding the confidence your user community has in relevant data.

BI Governance Step #3 - Enhance

The results of the monitor step will undoubtedly uncover multiple opportunities to enhance or start "cleaning up" the data. Analyzing queries running against analytical databases (even from multiple BI platforms) will yield identification of duplicate or near-duplicate queries—an opportunity to identify the culprits and consolidate duplicate, redundant, and

---

[53] Ibid.

[54] Bennett, Martha, Boris Evelson, Holger Kisker, and Carmen Stoica. "BI on BI: How To Manage The Performance of BI Initiatives."

overlapping BI content. Query analysis may also lead to an opportunity to optimize SQL and make queries perform better. Searching through and analyzing BI platform metadata may uncover business users' self-authored calculated metrics with formulas that deviate from enterprise-standard calculations—another opportunity for cleanup.

BI Governance Step #4 - Harden
Using a defined process established between business and IT, this step takes your users' self-authored applications often constructed from one or more data extracts and gradually repoints them to a central repository of curated content.

BI Governance Step #5 - Re-architect
Once in a while, the BI governance process may reveal a business-user, self-authored, mission-critical application that won't scale based on the number and complexity of data sources, the complexity of data preparation steps, frequency of refresh, data volumes, or the number of colleagues who use the application. In this instance, it may make sense to re-architect the application for enterprise scale.

Like Forrester, I recommend you take a phased approach to deploying BI governance.

First, assign BI governance roles and responsibilities to your BI and analytics competency center. If you don't have one, create one. Then make BI governance one of its primary responsibilities. Be sure to establish a strong working relationship with your data governance organization, too. Remember, the work you do in BI governance will inform data governance policies and best practices.

Next, get a quantitative view into your BI current state by deploying BI on BI. "There's no management without measurement" is a popular MBA program statement. This decades-old axiom directly applies to BI governance. BI on BI should be the cornerstone of your BI governance program.

Finally, work with IT to create policies and procedures for the enhance, harden, and re-architect steps of the BI governance process.

PERSPECTIVES FROM THE PROS

Mike Sargo

Today, with self-service tools, IT's role in business intelligence is fundamentally changing. Technology teams are now being tasked with supporting business stakeholders by designing and building data models rather than reports, and that's a good and necessary thing. Too often IT spends extensive, non-value-added time trying to understand user requirements and endlessly iterating through report and dashboard modifications. In many shops, this occurs with little oversight or governance. It's truly chaotic and a real cost to those organizations. With self-service, IT now has an opportunity to do what it does best—support the business as a trusted data advisor and data management organization. Contrary to the notion that IT is losing control, the data management professionals get to play an increasingly important value-added role. I believe that as IT delivers a broader set of high-quality data models and associated advisory services to support the business, companies will see a reduction in the error-prone manual processes associates with shadow IT analytics. Instead, by business and IT working as self-service analytics partners under a lightweight and agreed upon governance framework, organizations will experience more sophisticated uses of data and more accurate, complete, and trustworthy reports.

THE TAKEAWAY

Anecdotal evidence shows significant benefit from deploying BI governance including better alignment and partnership between business and IT, fewer BI silos due to program's "monitor and adjust" approach, and a more efficient and effective BI environment. Done right, BI governance is an important business enabler and an effective way of avoiding self-service anarchy that can paralyze your organization.

SECTION IV
THE TECHNOLOGY DOMAIN

INSIGHT [16]

THE ROLE OF TECHNOLOGY

THE POINT: TECHNOLOGY IS IMPORTANT, BUT DON'T GET SIDETRACKED BY IT

I like to quip that "business intelligence has nothing to do with technology." It's a true and important statement when used in the right context, like Section I of this book. That said, self-service analytics wouldn't be possible without technology. In fact, building a best-in-class data and analytics capability requires a strong data architecture, a dedicated data organization, and analytics and information delivery services that support the organization's demand for actionable insight. So, it probably goes without saying that technology plays a necessary and vital role in helping you compete and win with self-service analytics.

The technology landscape and its related processes are vast and ever-changing. For a big picture view, take a look at Matt Turck's latest Big Data Landscape.[55] In the meantime, here's a collection of some relevant terms you should know.[56] Consider it a time-

---

[55] Visit http://mattturck.com/bigdata2017/.
[56] Unless otherwise noted, all definitions are from *TechTarget* at http://whatis.techtarget.com.

saving ready-reference you can use to align stakeholders across your organization.

Artificial intelligence (AI) is the simulation of human intelligence by machines.

Big data is an evolving term that describes any voluminous amount of structured, semi structured and unstructured data that has the potential to be mined for information.

Big data as a service (BDaaS) is the delivery of statistical analysis tools or information by an outside provider that helps organizations understand and use insights gained from large information sets in order to gain a competitive advantage.

Cloud computing is a general term for the delivery of hosted services over the internet.

Data integration is the process of retrieving data from multiple source systems and combining it in such a way that it can yield consistent, comprehensive, current and correct information for business reporting and analysis.

Data preparation is the process of gathering, combining, structuring and organizing data so it can be analyzed as part of data visualization, analytics and machine learning applications.

A **data lake** is a storage repository that holds a vast amount of raw data in its native format until it is needed.

A **data mart** is a repository of data gathered from operational data and other sources that is designed to serve a particular community of knowledge workers.

Data visualization is a general term that describes any effort to help people understand the significance of data by placing it in a visual context.

A **data warehouse** is a central repository for all or significant parts of the data that an enterprise's various business systems collect.

An **enterprise data hub,** also referred to as a **data lake**, is a new big data management model for big data that utilizes Hadoop as the central data repository.

A **graph database,** also called a graph-oriented database, is a type of NoSQL database that uses graph theory to store, map and query relationships.

Hadoop is an open source distributed processing framework that manages data processing and storage for big data applications running in clustered systems.

An **in-memory database** is a type of analytic database designed to streamline the work involved in processing queries.

The **Internet of Things** (IoT) is a system of interrelated computing devices, mechanical and digital machines, objects, animals or people that are provided with unique identifiers and the ability to transfer data over a network without requiring human-to-human or human-to-computer interaction.

Machine learning (ML) is a category of algorithm that allows software applications to become more accurate in predicting outcomes without being explicitly programmed.

MPP database (massively parallel processing database) is a database that is optimized to be processed in parallel for many operations to be performed by many processing units at a time.

Natural language processing (NLP) is the ability of a computer program to understand human language as it is spoken.

NewSQL is a term coined by the analyst firm The 451 Group as shorthand to describe vendors of new, scalable, high performance SQL databases.

NoSQL (Not Only SQL database) is an approach to database design that can accommodate a wide variety of data models, including key-value, document, columnar and graph formats.

Robotic process automation (RPA) is an application of technology, governed by business logic and structured inputs, aimed at automating business processes. Using RPA tools, a company can configure software, or a "robot," to capture and interpret applications for processing a transaction, manipulating data, triggering responses and communicating with other digital systems.[57]

---

[57] Boulton, Clint. "What is RPA? A revolution in business process automation." *CIO*. 25 May 2018. (http://goo.gl/ib9NVF).

THE TAKEAWAY

A stable and high-performing technology infrastructure is important for self-service analytics to work. The landscape, though, is enormous and still growing. Don't get side-tracked and overwhelmed. Just be aware of what's out there, and stay focused on what you need to know when you need to know it.

INSIGHT [17]

THE SELF-SERVICE ARCHITECTURE

THE POINT: BUSINESS USERS HAVE A RESPONSIBILITY TO MITIGATE THE RISKS OF THE SELF-SERVICE ARCHITECTURE

You already know that self-service analytics is at the end of an often complex (and sometimes confusing) process that collects, prepares, and persists data for reporting and analysis. In fact, a lot goes on behind the scenes to create, manage, and support this data pipeline. Doug Kanouff, director of enterprise architecture for KeyBank, calls it a data factory. It's a great analogy, for one, because it makes the process easy to understand for non-technical folks: data enters as raw material, undergoes some processing along the way, and ends up in finished goods inventory ready for end-user consumption. It's a great analogy, too, because it connotates the real complexities associated with running a production line. If you've ever worked in a manufacturing facility, you know what I'm talking about. Logistical, technological, organizational, and environmental challenges—always hidden from the consumer's view—can make a plant manager's head spin. It's no different with the data factory, where enormous volumes of raw material from a myriad of suppliers pass through automated work centers that prepare, route, and deliver it for further end-user processing. In the data world, these "finished" and "semi-finished" goods could land in an integration services repository to support operational systems, a data warehouse for descriptive, diagnostic, and predictive analytics, or a subject-matter data mart to support regulatory reporting.

I could continue the factory metaphor, but you get the point. An effective self-service architecture blends one or more governed repositories of staged, integrated data created by IT with self-service data preparation and analytics capability used by the business. This kind of architecture gives designated business users the flexibility to source and further prepare their own data from anywhere in the data pipeline as business needs dictate without having to wait on IT. This independence and agility are a real benefit to the business and a necessary part of an effective self-service capability. However, the capability does come with risks. I want to give you some tips to help you mitigate them.

Risk Mitigation Tip #1 - Be aware of the cost

When organizations embark on self-service, the effort typically manifests itself in departmental users working to eliminate their reliance on IT. This often occurs when the business need for data outpaces the capacity of IT. Only later, though, do business leaders realize some of the unintended consequences of that very tactical thinking—like uncontrolled data proliferation, duplicative reports, and conflicting metrics. You need to understand that these and other consequences are costly to your organization. Some, like data proliferation and duplicative reports, are relatively easy to quantify by ascertaining extra storage cost and wasted labor hours. The issue of conflicting metrics is a bit more intangible but, suffice to say, any business decision made on wrong or suspect data can have a catastrophic effect.

Risk Mitigation Tip #2 - Partner-up

One of the ways to help mitigate the risks of self-service analytics is for the business and IT organizations to build a collaborative partnership. Work together to define primary points of contact—conduits to subject matter experts on the business side and various data management experts throughout IT. Document the details of data you source from outside of the governed repositories and share it with your colleagues. And work together to create a plan for hardening your self-service processes, when appropriate, into the mainstream data pipeline.

Risk Mitigation Tip #3 - Create an affinity group

An affinity group is a group of people linked by a common purpose. Consider establishing an affinity group of self-service analytics users to strategize on best practices, to understand the portfolio of intellectual capital that exists around the organization, to reuse (rather than recreate) existing data and reporting assets, and to plan ways to support established data governance policies in order to avoid unnecessary cost and operational risk.

PERSPECTIVES FROM THE PROS

Sri Seepana

The right self-service architecture provides business users who often have limited background and experience in technology or statistics with intuitive, user-friendly tools for reporting and analytics purposes. They are also given ownership and control over their data marts. These capabilities are then supported by infrastructure components that truly enable competitive advantage: an enterprise-level SOA framework, multiple layers of security, the ability to perform and scale based on evolving business needs, disaster recovery, and governance policies and procedures. This kind of environment can only result from a collaborative partnership between and IT.

THE TAKEAWAY

Business users don't own the self-service architecture, but they play a vital role in controlling the cost and mitigating the risks associated with it. Start by putting on a company lens. Think "big picture." Then simply follow my Risk Mitigation Tips to build some momentum.

INSIGHT [18]

THE PLACE FOR BIG DATA

THE POINT: BIG DATA PROVIDES A BIG OPPORTUNITY FOR DISCOVERY AND INSIGHT

"In a tech startup industry that loves shiny new objects, the term 'Big Data' is in the unenviable position of sounding increasingly '3 years ago.'"[58] That was Matt Turck in early 2016. Matt is a Managing Director of FirstMark Capital where he invests across a broad range of early-stage enterprise and consumer startups. Prior to FirstMark, he was a Managing Director at Bloomberg Ventures. Mr. Turck's blog post was intriguing for a variety of reasons and I encourage you to read it. I found it helpful in understanding what big data is (at least from Mr. Turck's point-of-view) and its future role in analytics. Here are the salient points excerpted from the post:

1. **"Big Data, fundamentally, is plumbing.** Certainly, Big Data powers many consumer or business user experiences, but at its core, it is *enterprise* technology:

---

58 "Matt Turck's Blog." Is Big Data Still a Thing? 1 Feb. 2016. (http://goo.gl/ih7NfQ).

databases, analytics, etc.: stuff that runs in the back that no one but a few get to see.

2. **Big Data success is not about implementing one piece of technology (like Hadoop or anything else), but instead requires putting together an assembly line of technologies, people, and processes.** You need to capture data, store data, clean data, query data, analyze data, visualize data.

3. **AI is not helping Big Data deliver on its promise.** The increasing focus on AI/machine learning in analytics corresponds to the logical next step of the evolution of Big Data: now that I have all this data, what insights am I going to extract from it?

4. **In many ways, we're still in the early innings of the Big Data phenomenon.** Building the infrastructure to store and process massive amounts of data was just the first phase. The combination of Big Data and AI will drive incredible innovation across pretty much every industry. From that perspective, the Big Data opportunity is probably even bigger than people thought."

So, know that big data is a big deal, and your ability to exploit it is an increasingly important means of competitive advantage. Here are my tips to help you prepare:

Big Data Tip #1 - Don't get distracted
Nearly everywhere you turn you find a technology-centric view of big data. When you hear big data, just think data. Ignore the host of definitions you come across and forget the 3 Vs: Volume, Variety, and Velocity. Remember, instead, Bill

Schmarzo's business-centric counterpoint called the 4 Ms of big data: Make Me More Money.

Big Data Tip #2 - Stay grounded

The promise of big data is big, but it's important that you ignore the hype. As McKinsey reports, success has been limited. "Very few have achieved what we would call 'big impact through big data,' or impact at scale."[59] Proceed with caution. Getting big data projects to production remains a big challenge.

Big Data Tip #3 - Make a plan

An effective plan promotes strategic dialogue at the top of the company and helps to shape investment priorities and to establish trade-offs. Your plan should address the preparation of extraordinary volumes of data, the selection of advanced analytic models that mine that data, and the creation of intuitive tools that translate the output of models into real business action.[60]

Through big data, forward-looking organizations have exciting opportunities to gain a level of insight into customers, markets, and products never before thought possible. And McKinsey believes that big data will become the key basis of greater competition, growth, and productivity. It's time to prepare.

---

[59] Court, David. "Getting big impact from big data." McKinsey Quarterly. Jan. 2015. (http://goo.gl/dQnssd).

[60] Biesdorf, Stefan, David Court, and Paul Willmott. "Big data: What's your plan?" McKinsey Quarterly. Mar. 2013. (http://goo.gl/nxBnNb).

PERSPECTIVES FROM THE PROS

Mike Sargo

Big data is one of the most overused and misunderstood terms in the business intelligence lexicon. In fact, for many organizations, it's the go to remedy for whatever ails them. In reality, very few have a business problem calling for a big data solution. Big data will certainly have its place in the future of BI as organizations look to modernize and expand their analytics capabilities. Some already are. But, if your firm is like most, you don't yet have a compelling use case that drives a significant, "must have" opportunity with big data. So, focus instead on maturing your current business intelligence implementation so that you can maximize its value. I work with many organizations that inevitably feel that they have a big data problem or project when in reality very few of them are actually focused on a problem that requires a big data solution to solve. There are many definitions for big data and the definition is continually evolving as tools and capabilities mature

THE TAKEAWAY

Organizations have access to more data now than ever before. But, in my experience, deriving meaningful and actionable insight from it is easier said than done. So, proceed with caution. Keep big data on your radar, and be on the lookout for opportunities that will certainly arise. But don't get distracted or side-tracked by all of the hype. Instead, focus your time and energy on perfecting a self-service analytics capability that really works and is prepared for big data when the time is right.

INSIGHT [19]

THE CONFUSING ANALYTICS LANDSCAPE

THE POINT: WE'RE NOT AS DUMB AS WE SOMETIMES FEEL

If your organization is like most (and it probably is), you can't attend a business meeting or have a hallway conversation without someone bringing up AI, RPA, or one of a host of other technology innovations that promise transformational change in the way business gets done. But, like the guy in the cartoon, it's really the excitement over potential benefit—and perhaps a fear of being left behind—that often drives our push to "do something." Problem is, the guy in the cartoon is a little confused. Maybe you feel that way sometimes, too. I certainly do.

With literally hundreds of software and platform vendors, tech start-ups, and consulting firms pitching their wares, it's hard for anyone to get a grasp on the analytics landscape—to truly understand one capability from another. Throw in research from analyst groups and a multitude of stories from the popular media (everyone has an opinion), all you get is a complicated mess. It's understandable, then, that the guy in the cartoon confused AI with robots. If you've done something similar, rest assured: you're not alone!

Like the technology landscape I covered earlier, the analytics landscape is vast. I've identified and summarized here the critical terms and capabilities I believe you should know and understand as you mature your self-service analytics capability. My intent, as always, is to keep things as simple as possible in order to provide needed clarity.

An **algorithm** is a step by step method of solving a problem. It is commonly used for data processing, calculation and other related computer and mathematical operations.[61]

Artificial intelligence (AI) is an area of computer science that emphasizes the creation of intelligent machines that work

---

[61] "Algorithm." *Techopedia*. (http://goo.gl/PHzsSK).

and react like humans.[62] How will you recognize AI? When a computer can convince a human that he's communicating with another human (Alan Turig, 1950). For a deeper and fascinating look into the definition of AI, check out a post by Bill Vorhies, editorial director for Data Science Central and a practicing data scientist since 2001.[63]

Cognitive computing is the simulation of human thought processes in a computerized model.[64] "Cognitive computing represents self-learning systems that utilize machine learning models to mimic the way [the] brain works. Eventually, this technology will facilitate the creation of automated IT models which are capable of solving problems without human assistance. Cognitive computing models provide a realistic roadmap to [achieving] artificial intelligence.[65] For a deeper dive into cognitive computing including its features, scope, and limitations, visit MarutiTech Labs.[66]

Ronald van Loon, considered one of the world's top influencers in data science and analytics, authored a recent article on cognitive computing.[67] In the LinkedIn Pulse post, he used the following graphic to illustrate the differences and overlap between cognitive computing and artificial intelligence.

---

[62] "Artificial intelligence." *Techopedia*. (http://goo.gl/JEQeBT).

[63] Visit http://www.datasciencecentral.com/profiles/blogs/what-exactly-is-artificial-intelligence-and-why-is-it-driving-me- or http://goo.gl/aEdPSz.

[64] "Cognitive computing." *SearchEnterpriseAI*. (http://goo.gl/24znbM).

[65] "What is cognitive computing?" Maruti Tech Labs. (http://goo.gl/LgoY1X):

[66] Visit http://www.marutitech.com/cognitive-computing-features-scope-limitations/ or http://goo.gl/LgoY1X.

[67] van Loon, Ronald. "Cognitive computing: Moving from Hype to Deployment." *LinkedIn Pulse*. 8 Feb. 2018. (http://goo.gl/sY1pbm).

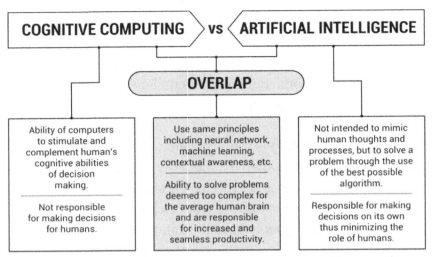

Figure 19.1 - Cognitive Computing vs. AI (Adapted from Ronald van Loon)

I find all of Ronald's work very helpful. You can subscribe to his YouTube channel at http://goo.gl/hhsA85 and follow him on Twitter at @Ronald_vanLoon.

Data science is the study of where information comes from, what it represents and how it can be turned into a valuable resource in the creation of business and IT strategies.[68] More specifically, the field of data science is emerging at the intersection of the fields of social science and statistics, information and computer science, and design.[69]

Data mining is the process of finding anomalies, patterns and correlations within large data sets to predict outcomes. As a discipline, data mining uses descriptive modeling, predictive modeling, and prescriptive modeling techniques to address a range of organizational needs, ask different types

---

[68] "Data science." *TechTarget*. (http://goo.gl/vDekCF).
[69] "What Is Data Science? A New Field Emerges." *Berkeley School of Information*. (http://goo.gl/2QzfBp).

of questions, and use varying levels of human input or rules to arrive at a decision.[70]

Deep-learning software attempts to mimic the activity in layers of neurons in the neocortex, the wrinkly 80 percent of the brain where thinking occurs. The software learns, in a very real sense, to recognize patterns in digital representations of sounds, images, and other data. The basic idea—that software can simulate the neocortex's large array of neurons in an artificial "neural network"—is decades old, and it has led to as many disappointments as breakthroughs. But because of improvements in mathematical formulas and increasingly powerful computers, computer scientists can now model many more layers of virtual neurons than ever before.[71]

DevOps is an approach to lean and agile software delivery that promotes closer collaboration between lines of business, development and IT operations. Historically, development and operations, and even testing, have been siloed operations. DevOps brings them together to improve agility and reduce the time needed to address customer feedback.[72] One of the primary benefits of DevOps is the continuous testing, release, deployment, and monitoring of software applications.

Distributed computing is a model in which components of a software system are shared among multiple computers to improve efficiency and performance.[73]

---

[70] "Data Mining: What Is it and why does it matter?" SAS Institute. (http://goo.gl/GSjP7i).

[71] Hoff, Robert. "Deep Learning." *MIT Technology Review*. 12 Jun. 2018. (http://goo.gl/z8YjNM).

[72] "What is DevOps?" *IBM*. (http://goo.gl/xjgHyB)

[73] "Distributed computing." *TechTarget*. (http://goo.gl/kyQsWC).

In artificial intelligence, an **expert system** is a computer system that emulates the decision-making ability of a human expert. Expert systems are designed to solve complex problems by reasoning through bodies of knowledge, represented mainly as if-then rules rather than through conventional procedural code.[74] One example of an expert system is an artificial intelligence system that emulates an auto mechanic's knowledge in diagnosing automobile problems.[75]

Machine learning is a method of data analysis that automates analytical model building. It is a branch of artificial intelligence and is based on the idea that systems can learn from data, identify patterns, and make decisions with minimal human intervention.[76]

Natural language processing (NLP) is a branch of artificial intelligence that helps computers understand, interpret and manipulate human language. NLP draws from many disciplines, including computer science and computational linguistics, in its pursuit to fill the gap between human communication and computer understanding.[77]

In information technology, a **neural network** is a system of hardware and/or software patterned after the operation of neurons in the human brain. Neural networks—also called

---

[74] "Expert system." *Wikipedia*. (http://goo.gl/ViTBNM).
[75] "What is an example of an expert system?" *Reference.com*. (http://goo.gl/njkpJv).
[76] "Machine Learning: What it is and why it matters." *SAS Institute*. (http://goo.gl/iHxhBw).
[77] "Natural Language Processing: What it is and why it matters" *SAS Institute*. (http://goo.gl/CZseMo).

artificial neural networks—are a variety of deep learning technologies.[78]

Robotic process automation (RPA) is the use of software with artificial intelligence (AI) and machine learning (ML) capabilities to handle high-volume, repeatable tasks that previously required humans to perform.[79]

Supervised (machine) learning is where you have input variables (x) and an output variable (Y), and you use an algorithm to learn the mapping function from the input to the output. The goal is to approximate the mapping function so well that when you have new input data (x) you can predict the output variables (Y) for that data. It is called supervised learning because the process of an algorithm learning from the training dataset can be thought of as a teacher supervising the learning process. We know the correct answers; the algorithm iteratively makes predictions on the training data and is corrected by the teacher.[80]

Unsupervised (machine) learning is where you only have input data (X) and no corresponding output variables. The goal of unsupervised learning is to model the underlying structure or distribution in the data in order to learn more about the data. This is called unsupervised learning because, unlike supervised learning, there are no correct answers and there is no teacher. Algorithms are left to their own devices,

[78] "Neural network." *TechTarget*. (http://goo.gl/ejNUyB).
[79] "Robotic process automation." *TechTarget*. (http://goo.gl/rvB9sR).
[80] Brownlee, Jason. "Supervised and Unsupervised Machine Learning Algorithms." *Machine Learning Mastery*. 16 Mar. 2016. (http://goo.gl/Bb17KZ).

so to speak, to discover and present the interesting structure in the data.[81]

Text mining, also known as **text analytics**, is the process of exploring and analyzing large amounts of unstructured text data aided by software that can identify concepts, patterns, topics, keywords and other attributes in the data.[82]

THE TAKEAWAY

As you can see, the analytics landscape can be challenging to navigate. The definitions provided here are a starting point, intended to help you build a foundational understanding of the technologies and capabilities. You can even use them to help align the many varying and disparate opinions that exist throughout your organization.

---

[81] Ibid.
[82] "Text mining (text analytics)." TechTarget. (http://goo.gl/uGv13T).

SECTION V

THE DATA DOMAIN

INSIGHT [20]

UNDERSTANDING DATA

THE POINT: EMPOWER USERS BY MAKING THEM DATA LITERATE

Your ability to compete and win with self-service analytics is dependent on your organization doing three things exceptionally well:

1. Providing faster, easier access to data
2. Deploying the right technology to consume it
3. Empowering more and more people to use it

But none of this really matters, though, if the user community isn't data literate. "Most companies recognize data in the hands of a few data experts can be powerful," writes Forbes contributor Brent Dykes. "But data at the fingertips of many is what will be truly transformational."[83] (Notice the important distinction between his use of "can" and "will.") In a recent article entitled, "Why Companies Must Close The Data Literacy Divide," Mr.

---

[83] Dykes, Brent. "Why Companies Must Close The Data Literacy Divide." *Forbes*. 9 Mar. 2017. (http://goo.gl/hgicS1).

Dykes makes an important point: "As organizations look to increase data access for their managers and employees, there's an implied expectation that they will know what to do with the data once it's shared with them." However, many companies are discovering—perhaps even yours—that democratizing data and providing tools to consume it simply aren't adequate. There's a critical "data literacy divide," as Dykes illustrates in Figure 20.1 below, that threatens to impede the efforts of even the savviest organizations.

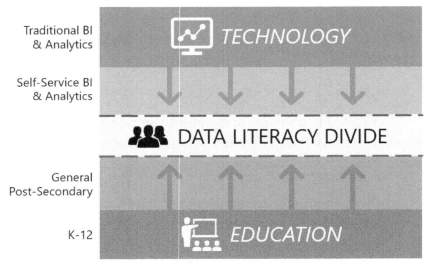

Figure 20.1 - The Data Literacy Divide (Courtesy of Brent Dykes)

So, what is "data literacy" anyway? Well, I like the simplicity of this definition:

> Data literacy is the ability to understand, use and communicate data effectively.[84]

---

84 Ibid.

In his article, Mr. Dykes outlines four areas of data literacy:

1. **Data knowledge**
   Each company, industry, and discipline have its own set of unique data terms and datasets. The more your users understand your company's data from a business perspective, the better positioned they are to apply it. This is also the area dealing with things like statistics fundamentals and understanding the difference between correlation and causation.

2. **Data assimilation**
   It's important that users orient themselves to unfamiliar data before consuming it. Data assimilation is all about understanding the characteristics of data. ChartMogul uses the acronym CAUSE to define the five characteristics of good data. Good data is Credible, Actionable, Unbiased, Statistically relevant, and Easy to interpret.[85]

3. **Data interpretation**
   After a user is familiar enough with the data, he should be able to analyze and interpret it. ChartMogul's cheat sheet is a great reference for remembering the twelve ways to "question data," (Figure 20.2) which chart type (Figure 20.3) and measure of central tendency to use, and tips like whether or not to truncate the Y axis.

4. **Data skepticism and curiosity**
   In addition to analyzing and interpreting data, users must also think critically about it. Too often data is accepted at

---

[85] "The Ultimate Data Literacy Cheat Sheet." ChartMogul. (http://goo.gl/i3YG5h).

face value. However, it's important to step back and weigh other less obvious factors that could influence the results and ultimate interpretation.

Take time to understand the extent to which your organization has a data literacy divide. Then take appropriate steps to remedy it. To get you started, Gartner has a website dedicated to data literacy including free research, a webinar, Gartner ThinkCast, and articles.[86] The firm also has toolkit to help you evaluate your current state and to enable data literacy and information as a second language.[87]

THE TAKEAWAY

"The emergence of data and analytics capabilities, including artificial intelligence, requires creators and consumers to 'speak data' as a common language," writes Valerie Logan, an analyst with Gartner. "Data and analytics leaders must champion workforce data literacy as an enabler of [the] digital business, and treat information as a second language."[88]

---

[86] Visit http://www.gartner.com/technology/research/data-literacy/ or http://goo.gl/FPV6ut.

[87] Visit http://www.gartner.com/doc/3810665/toolkit-enabling-data-literacy-information or http://goo.gl/r65WDD.

[88] Logan, Valerie. "Fostering Data Literacy and Information as a Second Language: A Gartner Trend Insight Report." Gartner, Inc., 23 Feb. 2018. (http://goo.gl/ZdDaW4).

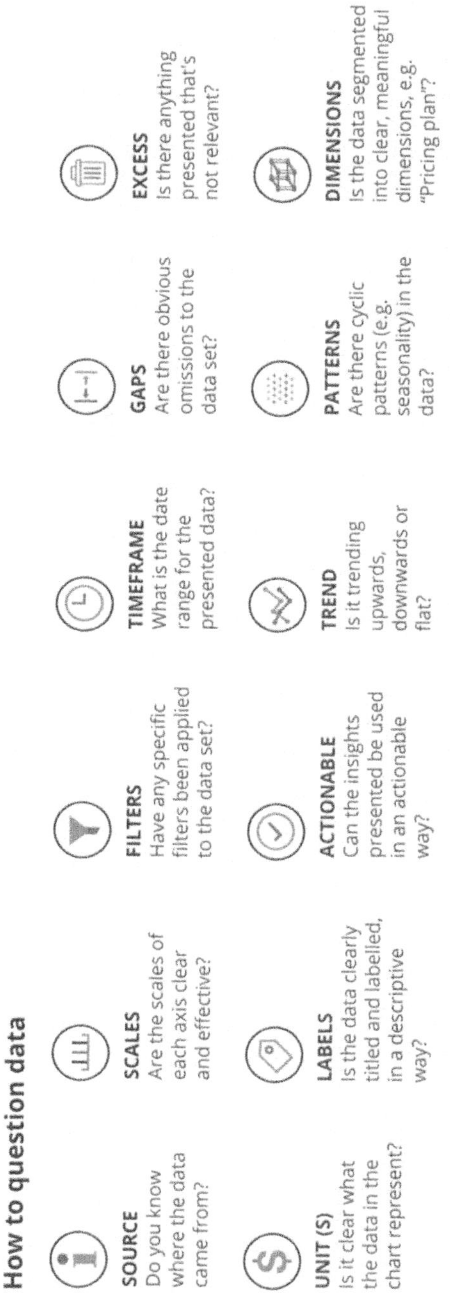

How to question data

SOURCE
Do you know where the data came from?

SCALES
Are the scales of each axis clear and effective?

FILTERS
Have any specific filters been applied to the data set?

TIMEFRAME
What is the date range for the presented data?

GAPS
Are there obvious omissions to the data set?

EXCESS
Is there anything presented that's not relevant?

UNIT (S)
Is it clear what the data in the chart represent?

LABELS
Is the data clearly titled and labelled, in a descriptive way?

ACTIONABLE
Can the insights presented be used in an actionable way?

TREND
Is it trending upwards, downwards or flat?

PATTERNS
Are there cyclic patterns (e.g. seasonality) in the data?

DIMENSIONS
Is the data segmented into clear, meaningful dimensions, e.g. "Pricing plan"?

Figure 20-2 - How to question data (Courtesy of ChartMogul)

Which chart should you use?

Comparing multiple values

Displaying the composition of a whole

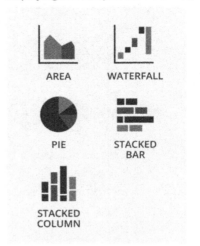

Showing distribution of values

Analyzing trends

Showing the relationship between sets

Figure 20.3 - Charts: Which one should you use? (Courtesy of ChartMogul)

INSIGHT [21]

PREPARING DATA

THE POINT: FOCUS ON THE 20/80 RULE

Most analytics professionals I speak with tell me they spend entirely too much time preparing data for analysis. In fact, with upwards of 80% of their time focused on data preparation and the other 20% of their time complaining about it, precious little time remains to actually use it. It's not an uncommon problem.

SearchBusinessAnalytics defines data preparation as "the process of gathering, combining, structuring and organizing data so it can be analyzed as part of data visualization, analytics, and machine learning applications."[89] Gartner describes it as the most time-consuming task in BI and analytics,[90] and I agree.

The rapid proliferation of data and the ever-increasing demand for analytics at the speed of business continue to propel self-service data preparation. Business leaders and the analysts that work for them can no longer afford the "luxury" of a centralized

---

[89] "Data preparation." SearchBusinessAnalytics. (http://goo.gl/KDFQ8G).
[90] Zaidi, Ehtisham, Rita L. Sallam and Shubhangi Vashisth. "Market Guide for Data Preparation." Gartner, Inc., 14 Dec. 2017. (http://goo.gl/cXxQeM).

data warehouse where data is systematically integrated, transformed, and staged for consumption. The IT-centric processes used to create a data warehouse are often complex and expensive, and the resulting repository can require a high level of quality control and governance to make it useful for the masses. The data factory simply takes too long to convert raw material to finished goods. For many organizations, the entire process has grown incompatible with the speed and agility decision-makers now need to act.

Self-service data preparation is, in its basic form, a business-friendly form of ETL. Its primary user is a business analyst rather than someone in IT, and its purpose is to help "prepare" data for analysis. Data preparation might include combining data, cleansing it, de-duplicating it, aggregating it, or even re-shaping it into something new. Self-service data preparation tools reduce the time and complexity associated with these types of tasks and now even include machine learning capabilities to help guide the user.

One of the benefits of self-service data preparation is that it helps reduce the workload on an already stretched and overallocated IT organization; at the same time, it helps to improve the overall experience and satisfaction of business stakeholders. That's one of the reasons Gartner predicts that by 2020 self-service data preparation tools will be used in more than half of all new data integration efforts.[91]

But there are a couple of cautions.

---

[91] Ibid.

- **Pick the right use cases**

  Not every analytics problem is a fit for self-service data preparation. Sometimes you need the rigor and sophistication that come with an enterprise grade ETL tool. Users should avoid wasting unnecessary time trying to demonstrate their creative problem-solving skills. Instead, establish guidelines that help to align business and IT stakeholders around appropriateness-of-fit, and define an agreed-upon, agile process to help drive timely execution.

- **Avoid working in a silo**

  Many business analysts like the idea of being self-sufficient, and data preparation tools can reinforce a "silo" mentality. Work hard to collaborate with your peers. In doing so, you can avoid costly redundancy and benefit from shared intellectual capital. Collaboration can also help to establish routine best practices and reduce unnecessary data proliferation

PERSPECTIVES FROM THE PROS

Sri Seepana

One of the hallmarks of self-service analytics is self-service data preparation, and self-service tools are fundamentally changing the dynamics between business and IT. On one hand, it's a good thing. IT can focus on core data management—something it does extremely well. Business users can focus on the speed and agility they need to act. On the other hand, a problem arises when either party thinks that self-service is the answer to any and every use case. It's not, and there's an important balancing act to play to ensure the enterprise reaps the rewards of the self-service strategy. In many instances, business needs data that is simply "good enough." And this perspective is fine for solving a lot of business problems—it aligns well with the function of self-service data preparation and the desire to get things done quickly. Sometimes, though, the quality and trust-worthiness of the data has to trump speed. Regulatory reporting and analysis is just one example. It is important that users are cognizant of the difference.

THE TAKEAWAY

The primary objective of self-service data preparation is to support speed-to-insight for appropriate use cases. Over time you should see a significant shift in the amount of time users allocate to analysis versus data preparation. You're trying to flip the equation from 80/20 to 20/80. If you don't see that kind of progress, you should probably re-evaluate your self-service data preparation strategy.

INSIGHT [22]

DATA ON THE EDGE

THE POINT: USE YOUR IMAGINATION TO DRIVE INNOVATION

Digital transformation is occurring everywhere—from major retailers and consumer packaged goods companies to hospitals and manufacturers. Using technology innovations like the Internet of Things (IoT), firms across industries are now beginning to drive new levels of performance and productivity.

"Edge" computing refers to the infrastructure that exists at the source of data. It could be wind turbine on a wind farm or a magnetic resonance imaging (MRI) machine in a hospital emergency room. The data generated by these machines is termed "data on the edge." It differs fundamentally from what we've always known about the Internet.

Timothy Chou, author and lecturer at Stanford notes that "Most technology we've built so far was for the Internet of People (IoP). Whether it was an e-commerce, ERP or search application, it was built to serve people—and to accumulate specific types of data that we could analyze later."[92] According to Chou, data collection has always followed problem identification. The IoT is changing that along with the assumptions about where, how and how quickly we can collect and manage data, analyze it, make predictions and do modeling.

"Everything generating data outside of a data center and connected to the Internet is at the edge," explains Oliver Schabenberger, Executive Vice President and Chief Technology Officer of SAS. "That includes appliances, machines, auto-mobiles, streetlights, smart devices in the home, turbines, locomotives, pets and healthcare equipment."[93] Traditionally, data is produced at the edge of the network and transported back to a data center where it's processed. Edge computing, on the other hand, processes the data at the source or the edge of the network.

Wikipedia defines Edge computing as "pushing the frontier of computing applications, data, and services away from centralized nodes to the logical extremes of a network.[94] It enables data gathering and analytics to occur at the source of the data.

But why is that important?

"For businesses, the most important benefit of the IoT will be the data generated by billions of new smart sensors and devices. The 'Internet of Everything'—all of the people and things connected to

---

[92] Turner, Cindy. "The future of IoT: On the edge." SAS Insights. 14 Jun. 2018. (http://goo.gl/rBC8hE).
[93] Ibid.
[94] "Edge computing." Wikipedia. (http://goo.gl/hZ3sBf).

the internet—will generate 507.5 zettabytes (1 zettabyte = 1 trillion gigabytes) of data by 2019, according to Cisco."[95]

In healthcare, for example, edge computing is becoming more and more popular as organizations introduce more connected medical devices into their health IT ecosystems.[96] In manufacturing, you can expect more than 50 billion devices connected by 2020 collecting an astronomical 1.4 billion data points per plant per day. But, as Kumar Balasubramanian, GM of Internet of Things Solutions at Intel explains, "Industries that stand to gain the most are those that are able to extract the right business insights at the right time and the right place—edge or cloud—based on factors like cost and latency of the underlying business problem."[97]

PERSPECTIVES FROM THE PROS

Mike Sargo

For those who are creative and aware, the Internet of Things (IoT) provides potential opportunity that morphs much of what we've seen in the world of analytics. The strategy of every organization should take it into account, even if it's something that's still a bit down the road from a practicality perspective. I've seen businesses achieve significant benefit from their investment in IoT, using data to solve problems that couldn't be addressed so easily otherwise. And there are countless use cases across a variety of industries. In healthcare, sensors are being installed in

---

[95] "Edge Computing in the IoT." *Business Insider*. 18 Oct. 2016. (http://goo.gl/iNjvFf).

[96] O'Dowd, Elizabeth. "Edge Computing Uses IoT Devices for Fast Health IT Analytics." *HIT Infrastructure*. 5 Apr. 2017. (http://goo.gl/uUssJJ).

[97] Turner, Cindy. "The future of IoT: On the edge."

almost every piece of new equipment being manufactured, and wearables are now being leveraged to proactively monitoring patient health and establish personalized care models. As the market continues to matures I would expect to see more organizations leverage IoT to drive what could be unprecedented value.

THE TAKEAWAY

Business intelligence practitioners should always be on the lookout for new and innovative ways to capture and analyze data. In many industries, data on the edge will enable fundamental transformation of whole business models. Business intelligence pros utilizing self-service analytics capabilities need to be prepared to leverage this exciting source of new data.

INSIGHT [23]

UNDERSTANDING DATA SCIENCE

THE POINT: DATA SCIENCE REALLY IS ABOUT THE SCIENCE OF DATA

It was October 2012 when Thomas Davenport labeled the data scientist as the sexiest job of the 21st century. At the time, the hype around big data was already near a fever pitch, and business leaders were looking for ways to capitalize on this "new and innovative thing." It was time to jump on the bandwagon. In his Harvard Business Review article, Mr. Davenport and his co-author, D.J. Patil describe the data scientist as "a high-ranking professional with the training and curiosity to make discoveries in the world of big data."[98]

Well, today, it's no longer "big" data. It's just data. And every business is in the data business. But, contrary to popular belief, not every BI professional or data analyst "does data science."

---

[98] Davenport, Thomas H. and D.J. Patil. "Data Scientist: The Sexiest Job of the 21st Century." *Harvard Business Review*. (http://goo.gl/2FEGxm).

141

The Data Science Association defines data science as "the scientific study of the creation, validation and transformation of data to create meaning."[99] Opinions on this differ, but it appears the term was originally coined in 1998 by statistician Chien-Fu Jeff Wu during his inaugural lecture at the University of Michigan. Wu argued that statisticians should be renamed data scientists since they spent most of their time manipulating and experimenting with data.[100]

Then, in 2014, Davenport wrote in a Wall Street Journal article that it's time to kill the title. "It [now] has as much ambiguity as the term big data."[101] Mr. Davenport commented that he saw the signs coming. "Shortly after the [Harvard Business Review] article came out," he wrote, "a woman introduced herself to me at a health care analytics conference. Her business card said 'Data Scientist,' but it was clear that she was a quantitative analyst at best. 'Who can resist having the sexiest job of the century?', she asked." Davenport wasn't impressed. The term data scientist had come to mean almost anything.

Mic Farris, a data science leader and member of IIA's expert network, penned an interesting LinkedIn Pulse blog entitled, "The Fundamentals of Data Science."[102] In it he outlines 10 "scientific" methods used by data scientists to achieve an organization's goals with data. Here's a summary excerpted from that post that I think is helpful in differentiating common business analytics from the world of data science.

---

[99] "Data science." *Data Science Association.* (http://goo.gl/gXem1G).

[100] Kuonen, Dr. Diego. "A Swiss Statistician's Big Tent View On Big Data and Data Science Version 10." Slideshare. (http://goo.gl/4piKWf).

[101] Davenport, Thomas H. "It's Already Time to Kill the "Data Scientist" Title." *The Wall Street Journal.* 30 Apr. 2014. (http://goo.gl/F4cBAw).

[102] Farris, Mic. "The Fundaments of Data Science." LinkedIn Pulse. 11 Sep. 2015. (http://goo.gl/M6wYoz).

1. **Probability and statistics**
    The world is a probabilistic one, so we work with data that is probabilistic—meaning that, given a certain set of pre-conditions, data will appear to you in a specific way only part of the time. To apply data science properly, one must become familiar and comfortable with probability and statistics.

2. **Decision theory**
    Decision theory is one of the key fundamentals of data science. Whether applied in the scientific, engineering, or business fields, we are trying to make decisions using data. Data itself isn't useful unless it's telling us something, which means we're making a decision about what it is telling us. How do we come up with those decisions? What are the factors that go into this decision-making process? What is the best method for making decisions with data?

3. **Estimation theory**
    Sometimes we make characterizations of data: averages, parameter estimates, etc. Estimation from data is essentially an extension of decision making, a natural next step from decision theory.

4. **Coordinate systems**
    To bring various data elements together into a common decision-making framework, we need to know how to align the data. Knowledge of coordinate systems and how they are used becomes important to lay a solid foundation for bringing disparate data together.

5. **Linear transformations**

   Once we understand coordinate systems, we can learn why to transform the data to get at the underlying information. This area describes how we can transform our data into other useful data products through various types of transformations, including the popular Fourier transform.

6. **Effects of computation on data**

   An often-overlooked aspect of data science is the impact the algorithms we apply have on the information we are seeking to find. Merely applying algorithms and computations to create analytics and other data products has an impact on the effectiveness of data-driven decision-making ability.

7. **Prototype coding/programming**

   One of the key elements to data science is the willingness of practitioners to "get their hands dirty" with data. This means being able to write programs that access, process, and visualize data in important languages in science and industry.

8. **Graph theory**

   Graphs are ways to illustrate connections between different data elements, and they are important in today's inter-connected world.

9. **Algorithms**

   Key to data science is understanding the use of algorithms to compute important data-derived metrics.

10. Machine learning

No fundamental understanding of data science would be complete without knowledge of machine learning.

PERSPECTIVES FROM THE PROS

Mike Sargo

Data science is all about extracting meaningful insight from vast amounts of information by leveraging a combination of mathematical and statistical analytics techniques. This type of work requires someone who really understands how to capture and interrogate the right data—"big or small"—in order to uncover meaningful and actionable insight, and to tell a compelling story about it. So, data science is a very important aspect of a comprehensive business intelligence capability. and should be a component that is thoughtfully incorporated into many business intelligence programs. That said, finding the right people can be challenging. Modernization efforts and the desire to exploit growing data volumes have increased market demand and, at the same time, raised concerns across the industry that there will be a very real shortage of data scientists. I do believe, though, that as business intelligence and analytics tools continue to evolve— like Tableau acquiring Empirical Systems, the AI startup out of MIT—we'll find more and more BI "generalists" acting in the role of citizen data scientist.

THE TAKEAWAY

As Dr. Kuonen points out, data science is more a rebranding of data mining than anything that bears resemblance to traditional business intelligence, business analytics or, as Tom Davenport laments, even quantitative analytics. Perhaps advancements in technology that now enable traditional analysts to do the kind of work once reserved for specialists is causing a sea change. In any case, understanding both the complexities and nuances associated with data science is an important undertaking.

INSIGHT [24]

DATA PRIVACY

THE POINT: KNOW THE LAW

Data Privacy Day is an international event observed each January 28 to create awareness around information sharing and the importance of safeguarding data. According to StaySafeOnline.org, the event began in the United States and Canada in 2008 as an extension of Europe's Data Protection Day which commemorates the first legally-binding international treaty dealing with privacy and data protection.

Data privacy, also referred to as information privacy, deals with the collection of data and the ability of an individual or organization to determine its access and dissemination. Privacy concerns exist wherever personally identifiable information (PII) or other sensitive personal or corporate information is collected, stored, used, and ultimately destroyed.

TechTarget defines a data breach as "a confirmed incident in which sensitive, confidential or otherwise protected data has been accessed and/or disclosed in an unauthorized fashion." Data breaches may impact an individual's privacy through personal health information (PHI) or personally identifiable information (PII); or they could impact corporate entities through the compromise of trade secrets or intellectual property. Consumer breaches, though, are the most visible and can have a catastrophic impact on the lives of individuals and families. Some of the most notable data breaches include retail giant Target Corporation in 2013, Sony Pictures Entertainment in 2014, Yahoo in 2013 and 2014, and even the Office of Personnel Management (OPM) in 2015.

To help protect consumers, the United States has enacted numerous laws and compliance regulations pertaining to privacy, including the well-known Health Insurance Portability and Accountability Act (HIPAA) that helps ensure patient confidentiality associated with healthcare-related data. In banking, the Gramm-Leach-Bliley Act mandates how financial institutions deal with the private information of individuals. The topic is of such great importance that data protection rules in Europe have undergone the biggest change in nearly two decades. The General Data Protection Regulation, or GDPR, overhauls how businesses process and handle the vast amounts of personal data created each and every day. GDPR is expected to impact privacy regulations around the world.

The privacy landscape is complex and can be confusing. Laws vary by country, state, and industry, and fines for running afoul of regulations can be significant. According to information-age.com, "the first six months of 2017 saw more data lost or stolen than throughout the whole of 2016. A 2017 Cost of Data Breach Study conducted by Ponemon pegs the average cost of a breach at $3.62 million. But the negative impact on business goes beyond the financials. In one of the biggest impacts on a company following a data breach is its reputation. According to Entrepreneur, studies indicate that up to a third of customers in retail, finance and healthcare will stop doing business with organizations that have been breached.

The Takeaway

It's the duty of every analytics professional to understand data privacy—to know what is and isn't permissible. Know the law. Make sure you understand your employer's policies, procedures, and guidelines that govern your work. Be diligent about safeguarding data, and know who to call when you suspect a privacy breach. Don't take this responsibility lightly.

SECTION VI

CLOSING THOUGHTS

INSIGHT [25]

PLANNING AND EXECUTION

THE POINT: PLAN FOR ACCELERATED EXECUTION

Planning is preparation for action. If you are going to deliver data that is relevant, information that is meaningful, and insight that is actionable, your execution has to be fast and it has to be focused. It also has to be built on a foundation of solid planning. The purpose of planning is to:

1. Empower the self-service analytics community by instilling principles that guide the right behavior for the benefit of the enterprise;
2. Ensure you to take all known and relevant information into account so you can help to future-proof work effort by maximizing reuse and minimizing rework of analytics deliverables.

Planning is the means to effective execution. In your quest to create the insight-driven enterprise, plan for accelerated execution by following these four guiding principles.

Guiding Principle #1 - Embrace agile principles

Familiarize yourself with the Twelve Principles of Agile Software[103] and make the concepts a part of the way you think. They were established to satisfy the customer through early and continuous delivery of valuable software. Always remember that agility is driven by a desire to serve our customers in a relevant and responsive way.

Guiding Principle #2 - Under-promise, Over-deliver

Did you know that many of the unreasonable expectations we find ourselves managing are the direct result of things we say or unintended impressions we leave? That's been my experience. When we overcommit, we set ourselves up for failure. And nothing frustrates business users more than when we tell them one thing but do another. "Under-promise, over-deliver" is a best practice for planning because it helps you to set reasonable expectations. It's a best practice for execution, too, because it helps ensure you deliver on-target, on-budget, on-time, every time.

Guiding Principle #3 - Over-communicate

Nobody likes surprises, so set the stage early in your planning effort to communicate more than necessary more often than necessary. It's a practice that goes a long way to building trust and cooperative partnerships with people.

Guiding Principle #4 – Get organized

Your ability to be quick and nimble is tied to how well organized you are. Make sure you have the right tools at your disposal. Build a library of standard templates, scripts, and other artifacts you can reuse from one work effort to another

---

[103] "The Twelve Principles of Agile Software." Agile Alliance. (http://goo.gl/EymP1H).

so you don't waste valuable time. And then collaborate and share to help your colleagues get and stay organized, too.

THE TAKEAWAY

In business today, it is imperative that organizations find a way to capitalize on opportunities that surface from market disruption. In fact, a fiercely competitive business environment has led "agility" to trump "perfectly architected." It's a philosophy that certainly aligns well with self-service analytics. Just keep in mind that effective self-service doesn't just happen. It requires the right type of planning to drive nimble execution.

INSIGHT [26]
CHANGE IS INEVITABLE

**THE POINT: LEARN TO THINK FAST BECAUSE YOUR
SURVIVAL DEPENDS ON IT**

Organizations are living organisms. Those that effectively compete and win on analytics make continuous learning an ongoing part of their DNA. They work hard to foster an environment of real-time collaboration that enables them to capture and share the intellectual capital that exists across the enterprise. And they make the improvement of business and decision-making processes a way of life by replicating the successes of others and by learning from their own failures.

The need to lead in data and analytics is pervasive. After all, business leaders expect the significant investments they make in data infrastructure and analytics capability to yield significant results. Today. What many fail to realize, though, is that building a culture of analytics that ultimately drives competitive advantage is an evolutionary process.

Things change so fast. That's why you need to think fast. High-performing organizations are adaptive, fast-moving organizations that respond quickly and flexibly to opportunities as they arise. They confront challenges. They respond, adjust, and learn; then they do it again. High-performers evolve, and they must because their very survival depends on it.

McKinsey calls it the urgency imperative. "When you compete in a marketplace that moves so quickly, the default outcome is to fall behind. If your organization is to have any hope of keeping up, it will have to be reconceived (like a race car) as fast, quick to turn, and even quicker to emerge from rapid pit stops and tune-ups."[104]

Change is inevitable. The pace of change almost unfathomable. Self-service analytics works best when you expect change, when you plan for it, learn from it, and embrace it.

THE TAKEAWAY

Too often we think the work we do today will have long-lasting value. We view our efforts as "one and done." Well, we need to evolve our thinking. As McKinsey points out, speed is the objective function, the operating model, and the cultural bias at the highest-performing companies. They repeatedly use catch-phrases like "energy," "metabolic rate," "bias for action," and "clock speed." These organizations recognize the reality of change, and they relentlessly pursue the creation of value in the very midst of a market filled with chaos. They worship speed and agility.

Do you think and operate that way?

---

[104] De Smet, Aaron and Chris Gagnon. "Organizing for the age of urgency." *McKinsey Quarterly*. Jan. 2018. (http://goo.gl/Wv3NXQ).

OTHER PUBLICATIONS BY GREG STEFFINE

Hyper: Changing the way you think about, plan, and execute business intelligence for real results, real fast!

Sanderson Press
ISBN: 978-0692423080

Available in Kindle, paperback, and hard cover editions.

Foreword by Boris Evelson, Principal Analyst, Forrester Research, Inc.

2018 Top 30 Best Data Science Books - Data Science Programs Guide
2016 eLIT Gold Award - Best Business Reference Book
#1 Amazon Bestseller - Social Science Methodology (June 2018)
#1 Amazon Bestseller - Library and Information Science (June 2018)
#4 Amazon Bestseller - Organizational Change (February 2017)
#5 Amazon Bestseller - Management Information Systems (June 2018)
#7 Amazon Bestseller - Computer Literacy (June 2018)
#8 Amazon Bestseller - Knowledge Capital (June 2017)
#10 Amazon Bestseller - Information Management (December 2016)
Nominated for 2016 Small Business Book Award

Cover Design: Mayfly Design
Interior Design: The Book Designer
Cover Typography: Realtime Rounded
Interior Typography: Roboto Black, Roboto Regular, Roboto Condensed,
Theano Didot